I CAME TO PERFORM THE LAW

A STUDY ON THE MEANING OF *PLEROO* ("FULFILL") IN MATTHEW 5:17

I Came to Perform the Law: A Study on the Meaning of *Pleroo* ("Fulfill") in Matthew 5:17

Pronomian Publishing LLC
Clover, SC 29710

Published in the United States of America.

Eitan's analysis of Matthew 5:17–18 is well organized and presented in a methodical and robust manner. Taking into consideration all relevant scholars, history, and linguistics, Eitan shows that Torah continuity presents itself as the most consistent, coherent, corresponding, and comely conclusion. From these words of Christ we should interpret Paul.
—G. Scott McKenzie, Ph.D.

Eitan ben Levi is a growing voice within pronomian Christianity who, after years of being taught from the pulpit that the fulfillment of the Torah by Messiah Yeshua resulted in its laws being rendered inoperative, realized that this narrative ultimately deconstructs the doctrine of immutability. Through meticulous research and applying consistent hermeneutical principles, he systematically shows that God and His breathed out words are not bound by dispensation, but intended for all redeemed peoples, past, present and future. In fulfilling the Torah, the Son seeks for us to emulate Him and His commitment to the preserved will of the Father.
—Benjamin Szumskyj, Ph.D.

Contents

Abbreviations

English Versions of the Bible

KJV	King James Version
NASB95	New American Standard Version, 1995 Ed.

Greek Versions of the Bible

NA28	Nestle-Aland Novum Testamentum Graece, 28th Ed.

General Abbreviations

LXX	Septuagint
NT	New Testament
OT	Old Testament

Journals

AcT	*Acta Theologica*
Bib	*Biblica*
BibSac	*Bibliotheca Sacra*
CBQ	*Catholic Biblical Quarterly*
Di	*Dialog*
HTS	*Harvard Theological Studies*
IDS	*In die Skrflig*
JMT	*Journal of Ministry & Theology*
LASBF	*Liber Annuus*
TynBul	*Tyndale Bulletin*

Monographs and Commentaries

BECNT	Baker Exegetical Commentary on the New Testament
BTC	Brazos Theological Commentary on the Bible
ECNT	Exegetical Commentary on the New Testament

EGGNT	Exegetical Guide to the Greek New Testament
ICC	International Critical Commentary
NAC	New American Commentary
NTL	New Testament Library
TNTC	Tyndale New Testament Commentaries

Reference Works

BDAG	Danker, Frederick W., Walter Bauer, William F. Arndt, and F. Wilbur Gingrich. *A Greek–English Lexicon of the New Testament and Other Early Christian Literature*. 3rd ed. Chicago, IL: University of Chicago Press, 2000.
GELS	Muraoka, Takamitsu. *A Greek-English Lexicon of the Septuagint*. Leuven: Peeters, 2009.
HALOT	Koehler, Ludwig, and Walter Baumgartner. *The Hebrew and Aramaic Lexicon of the Old Testament*. Leiden, Netherlands: Koninklijke Brill NV, 2000.
L&N	Louw, Johannes P., and Eugene A. Nida, eds. *Greek-English Lexicon of the New Testament Based on Semantic Domains*. 2nd Ed. New York: United Bible Societies, 1996.
TDNT	Bromiley, Geoffrey W. *Theological Dictionary of the New Testament: Abridged in One Volume*. Grand Rapids, MI: William B. Eerdmans.

Foreward

Within the past 50 years or so, a theological debate has started to take shape. Many within the Church have come to believe the Law of God is something believers should be studying and practicing. This has been met with strong opposition from those who contend the Law of God was fulfilled when Christ died on the cross. Such theological disagreement has not been confined to scholarly conferences or the classrooms of seminaries, but most often starts within families and then moves into the Church. Often, pastors are the last to enter the debate after several families in the Church are swayed by pronomian theology.

Each side of the debate has passages they tend to favor. Those who believe the Law was nailed to the cross often bring up passages such as Mark 7:19, Colossians 2:16–17, or Acts 15:19–20, while those who contend believers should keep the Law point to texts like Romans 3:31, 1 John 3:4, and Acts 15:21. Yet, no matter the position taken, both sides inevitably return to a single passage. Each side of this debate at some point references Matthew 5:17–20.

For those who believe the Mosaic Law is still applicable today, they appeal to Matthew 5:17 to show that Jesus did not come to do away with the law. While those who oppose this view point to Jesus' statement that he came to "fulfill" the Law to show that it has come to an end. Within this framework, interpreters argue that Christ's work on the cross fulfilled everything and, therefore, did away with the Law for anyone who places their faith in Jesus. Yet those who believe the Law remains contend that all is not fulfilled until Christ sits on His throne in Jerusalem and everything is placed in subjection unto Him. For this passage, the debate hinges on the term "fulfill" and what Jesus meant when He said it.

The following work is vital for this debate, as it gets to the heart of the issue. Eitan ben Levi surveys the use of this word throughout the text of

Scripture and beyond to better understand the appropriate context and meaning we should attribute to Jesus' words. This passage is critical for both sides as it will speak to the rest of the debate on the place of Torah in the life of a believer. If Jesus intended for His audience to understand that the Torah was going to be fulfilled at His death and would no longer apply to His followers, the rest of the New Testament would need to be viewed with this interpretation in mind. However, if Jesus intended to say the Law and the Prophets would not pass away until the eschatological conclusion when Jesus physically sits on His throne and death and sin are destroyed, then the rest of the New Testament will need to be interpreted within this framework.

Eitan ben Levi's work is one of the key starting points for believers to better understand the larger debate. Understanding Jesus' words here will steer our theological understanding of sanctification and will give us a better understanding of Jesus and the Apostles' approach to the law of God.

—C. M. Hegg
Executive Director - TorahResource

Introduction

"The Law is Fulfilled"

The nature of the relationship between the Christian and the Torah (Law) is one that has, in recent times, seen renewed debate among Believers.[1] The great majority argue that the birth, death, and resurrection of Jesus (Yeshua) brought about radical changes in the way the Law applies to Christians by means of the inauguration of the New Covenant.[2] As such the Law, or at least the Civil and Ceremonial parts of it, is more useful as a source of spiritual truths than as a guide for the lifestyle of the redeemed.[3] In contrast, a minority primarily consisting of believers in the Messianic Jewish and Pronomian Christian movements argues that the Torah is a timeless covenant that was only influenced by Messiah's coming in the sense that the death and resurrection of Yeshua made visible the substance of atonement foreshadowed by the Torah. This, in turn, changed the function of Torah from being a harbinger of forthcoming redemption to a reminder of God's work of salvation in the death of Yeshua. It then logically follows for Messianics and Pronomians that the Torah deserves full obedience from Christians as a means of worship to the Redeemer.[4]

---

1 Philip la Grange Du Toit, "The Fulfillment of the Law According to Matthew 5:17: A Dialectical Approach," *AcT* 38, no. 2 (2018): 50.

2 Christians vary with respect to what time in Christ's work brought changes to the Torah. Some say it was His birth, others His life, others His death, and still others say it was the totality of Christ's work on Earth from birth to ascension. Nevertheless, what the majority do agree on is that Yeshua's work changed the way believers are expected to live before God.

3 The Rev. J. R. Dummeflow, ed., *A Commentary on the Holy Bible* (New York: MacMillan, 1909), 641.

4 Tim Hegg, *It Is Often Said: Vol. 4* (Tacoma, WA: TorahResource, 2013), 20.

In this debate, both sides have several key texts of Scripture which form the basis for each respective understanding. The majority view, which we will call the antinomian view, often appeals to such verses as John 1:17, Acts 15, and Heb 8:7, and the minority view, which we will call the pronomian view, often appeals to such passages as Acts 21, Rom 2:13, and James 2:14–18.[5]

Although both the antinomian and pronomian views have multiple proof-texts that can be cited in support of their respective positions, there is one scripture that stands in a unique position with respect to this debate: Matthew 5:17. This passage is unique for two reasons. First, it is a concise statement made by Christ concerning His view of the effects of His work on the Law. Second, both the antinomian and pronomian positions regularly appeal to this text in support of their opposing views. As such, the central question of this book is, *What is the correct interpretation of Matthew 5:17?* I will answer this question by consulting other places in the Gospels where Yeshua uses similar key words to see whether this passage better supports an antinomian or pronomian view of how Christians should relate to the Torah.

The Question of Fulfillment

Given that Matthew 5:17 is cited in support of opposite positions on the relationship between the Christian and the Torah, it is hardly surprising that pronomians interpret the verse with a meaning that is almost the exact opposite of the antinomian interpretation. Far more surprising in this regard is that the difference between the antinomian and pronomian interpretations of the passage hinges upon the meaning assigned to a single

5 Although in many Bible commentaries the word *antinomianism* is used to refer specifically to the belief that Christians are not even bound by so much as a code of ethics because of Jesus, I am not being so specific here. In this book, the term *antinomian* is used of any view that understands Jesus to have taken away the need for Christians to obey part or all of the Old Testament Law, the Torah.

word within the verse. The antinomian and pronomian interpretations are most sharply distinguished[6] by the meaning understood behind the Greek word πληρωσαι (pronounced *play-ro-sai*, but transliterated *plerosai*), an Aorist Active Infinitive from πληρόω (pronounced *play-ra-oh*, but transliterated *pleroo*) often rendered as "to fulfill" in English.[7]

Members of the antinomian persuasion understand πληρόω (*pleroo*) to mean that Yeshua did away with the need for His followers to obey the Torah, though there are diverse perspectives on whether this constitutes a wholesale or piecemeal abandonment.[8] Historically, the view that Christ abolished the Torah in its entirety has been dominant, but in the last few centuries competing theologies have suggested that the Torah was abolished only in part, or temporarily suspended during the church age.[9] What all members of this family of perspectives have in common, however, is their interpretation of πληρόω (*pleroo*), which they understand to carry a meaning along the lines of *bring to an end*, *transcend* or *obey*.[10] Thus, these perspectives assert that Yeshua's fulfillment of the Torah involves, on some level, damage to the relevance of the Torah for Christians. For brevity, I will call these interpretations of the meaning of πληρόω (*pleroo*) the *destructive* view.

Members of the pronomian persuasion interpret πληρόω (*pleroo*) in Matthew 5:17 as being primarily additive, understanding the word along

---

6 A few scholars do base their disagreements on how much of a role the contrast between "abolish" and "fulfill" should play for the verse's interpretation, but most of the debate centers around what "fulfill" is intended to mean.

7 BDAG, s.v. "πληρόω," 1:828.

8 Bradley M. Trout, "The Nature of the Law's Fulfilment in Matthew 5:17: An Exegetical and Theological Study," in *die Skrflig* 49, no. 1 (2015): 2–3.

9 Honore Sewakpo, "Jesus' Fulfillment of the Law in Mathew 5:17: A Panacea for Breaking the Law in Africa," *The Journal of Pan African Studies* 12, no. 5 (November 2018): 113.

10 David L. Turner, *Matthew*, BECNT (Grand Rapids, MI: Baker Academic, 2008), 157.

the lines of the English *establish*, *confirm*, *make whole*, or *uphold*.[11] As with the antinomian views, individual perspectives vary. Many who interpret πληρόω (*pleroo*) in this sense argue that Christ intended the Torah to be the foundation for the practice of the Church, but not all agree on this. Some scholars posit that the relationship of the Church to the Torah was debated in early Christianity, with Paul endorsing the antinomian view that would become normative within the church.[12] Others such as Mark Nanos argue that the first-century church understood the Law to be normative only for Jewish believers and not Gentiles.[13] Because all these views assign a similar meaning to πληρόω (*pleroo*), they will here be called the *constructive* view due to their common belief that the work of Yeshua builds on the Torah without damaging its relevance for believers.

Thus, in this passage there are two schools of thought: if you interpret πληρόω (*pleroo*) with a *destructive* or a *hybrid*[14] meaning, you will almost certainly have an antinomian view in general, likewise if you interpret πληρόω (*pleroo*) with a constructive meaning you will almost certainly have a pronomian outlook toward the rest of the Scriptures. With this said, there is one other important thing to note: by itself, Matthew 5:17 will not prove to us exactly how the Christian should relate to the Torah. Biblical doctrine should not be created in the vacuum of a single verse; rather, it should be based upon the harmonious message of many passages from throughout the Bible.

Despite the fact that this study will not aim to provide absolute resolution to the debate between the antinomian and pronomian views, the meaning of πληρόω (*pleroo*) is still a key we must utilize in order to

---

11 Du Toit, "Dialectical Approach," 50.

12 Thomas R. Schreiner, Luke Timothy Johnson, Douglas A. Campbell and Mark D. Nanos, *Four Views on the Apostle Paul* (Grand Rapids, MI: Zondervan, 2012), 117.

13 Schreiner, Johnson, Campbell and Nanos, *The Apostle Paul*, 167.

14 *Hybrid* interpretations of πληρόω (*pleroo*) combine the destructive and constructive meanings of the word, arguing that in some sense both meanings are in view.

correctly understand the Biblical evidence regarding Jesus' opinion of the Law. In this case, πληρόω (*pleroo*) as it appears in Matthew 5:17 is one of the relatively rare cases where Biblical doctrine is strongly affected by a single word of the Biblical text. As such, the precise meaning of πληρόω (*pleroo*) in Matthew 5:17 is a significant problem that must be addressed as a key step in understanding how the Bible teaches Christians to go about their daily lives. It is this purpose that I seek to address in this book by gathering a key piece of evidence that will support your thinking as you depart to study the rest of the Scriptures to see what else is written on this subject.[15]

The Purpose of This Book

While other scholars have attempted to resolve the meaning of Matthew 5:17 by various means, one relevant contextual study[16] that has been overlooked by scholars is a study of how Yeshua uses the Greek word πληρόω (*pleroo*) throughout the Gospels. While past studies have either assumed a given meaning for πληρόω (*pleroo*) or focused attention on its uses in Matthew's Gospel only, the study of πληρόω (*pleroo*) as used by Jesus will provide a more defensible clarification of how He uses the word in Matthew 5:17.[17]

By attempting to determine the most likely meaning of πληρόω (*pleroo*) without assuming a particular use in advance, this book will avoid the fallacy of circular reasoning into which some interpreters have fallen when it comes to Matthew 5:17.[18] Further, studying the uses of πληρόω

---

15 If you would like a more compact perspective on Matthew 5:17, see David Wilber, *How Jesus Fulfilled the Law: A Pronomian Pocket Guide to Matthew 5:17–20* (Clover, SC: Pronomian Publishing, 2024).

16 That is, a study performed on a particular group of related Biblical passages.

17 Bradley M. Trout, "Matthew 5:17 and Matthew's Community" *HTS* 72, no. 3 (2016): 2.

18 For example, see Dummeflow, *Commentary*, 641. This commentator subtly assumes his conclusions (that "fulfill" means Jesus changed the Law especially)

(*pleroo*) in the voice of a particular speaker as opposed to a particular Gospel will give my conclusion stronger support in two ways. First, as the instances of this word will be drawn from all four Gospels, the study will be able to assess the semantic range of πληρόω (*pleroo*) in some isolation from the emphases of each individual Gospel writer. Second, assessing the occurrences of the word as used by Jesus in reported speech will provide a useful means to exclude most of the less-relevant uses of πληρόω (*pleroo*). In this way, we will examine Matthew 5:17 and πληρόω (*pleroo*) specifically from an angle that has so far been largely ignored by scholarship, but our observations will offer some much-needed clarity on this section of the Sermon on the Mount.

The Goal of This Book

The end goal is to use the occurrences of πληρόω (*pleroo*) where the word is spoken by Jesus in all four Gospels as a contextual aid to determine the range of meanings for πληρόω (*pleroo*) as Yeshua used the word. This will show which contexts are most similar to Matthew 5:17 while having a clearer meaning, and ultimately this will reveal the most likely intended meaning of πληρόω (*pleroo*) in Matthew 5:17. While we will discover that it is difficult to point to any one scholar's work as the one and only correct interpretation of Matthew 5:17, we will discover evidence for a particular family of interpretations, and this will guide us in the right direction for discovering the exact meaning of Matthew 5:17.

Significance of the Fulfillment Debate

As we have noted previously, Matthew 5:17 is well-regarded as a key passage for understanding the precise relationship between Christ and the

---

in order to construct his argument to prove those same restated conclusions. This kind of thinking is called circular reasoning in logic, a type of logical fallacy.

Torah, and more broadly between the Torah and the Church. For this reason Matthew 5:17 has received heavy attention from scholars and pastors alike, each seeking to uncover the exact meaning expressed by Yeshua in this section of the Sermon on the Mount.[19] Why then is it necessary to engage in further study? The answer to this question is that, while Matthew 5:17 has been heavily analyzed in certain contexts, others have been neglected almost completely by scholarship, missing key details that can tip the scales of evidence in favor of one family of interpretations over another. As a result, the study you are about to embark on is significant for both theological and practical reasons, because it directly affects the traditions and practices of the modern Church.

Theological Significance

A study of the word πληρόω (*pleroo*) as it is used by Jesus is theologically significant because of its unique methodology. By examining πληρόω (*pleroo*) as it is used by a particular speaker across all four gospels, the study will be able to look beyond the emphases of each individual gospel writer, arriving at a conclusion regarding what πληρόω (*pleroo*) meant in the mind of Christ Himself. Discovery of this range of meaning for πληρόω (*pleroo*) as used by Yeshua is directly useful for our purposes, as this word is often used of the relationship between Christ and the Tanach (Old Testament).[20] This will help clarify not just what Yeshua thought of His relationship to the Torah, but also His relationship to the Messianic prophecies of the Tanach.

19 Trout, "Nature," 2.

20 J.R. Daniel Kirk, "Conceptualising Fulfillment in Matthew," *TynBul* 59, no. 1 (2008): 79–80.

Practical Significance

Perhaps more obvious, the study of πληρόω (*pleroo*) has extensive practical significance, for its appearance in Matthew 5:17 undergirds a significant statement regarding the Christian's relationship to the Torah and therefore is a significant statement regarding how a faithful Christian should conduct his or her personal and community life. If the word carries a destructive meaning, then traditional Christianity has, from the point of view of Matthew 5:17, been correct to reject the commandments of Torah on the grounds that they don't apply to the Christian. If, on the other hand, πληρόω (*pleroo*) carries a constructive sense, then Christ is expressly denying any rejection of the Torah and is simultaneously affirming that it should be embraced by the Christian Church as the Law by which believers are divinely governed in all aspects of life.[21] In this respect, demonstrating that πληρόω (*pleroo*) carries a constructive force in Matthew 5:17 would have a foundational impact on the traditional practices of the Church, and for you as a follower of Jesus.

What Do I Believe?

Before moving forward, my own position on the meaning of Matthew 5:17, and more broadly how the Torah relates to the Christian Church today, deserves to be disclosed. I believe that many of the conceptions out there on the meaning of πληρόω (*pleroo*) as it is used in Matthew 5:17 are flawed. The deepest flaw as best as I can see it in most popular interpretations is that they violate a cardinal rule of Christian Bible interpretation, namely that any proposed interpretation of the Bible should be consistent with both itself and with the broader witness of the Scriptures.[22] In particular, I believe that many interpretations of Matthew 5:17 are incon-

---

21 James H. Burtness, "Life-Style and Law: Some Reflections on Matthew 5:17," *Di 14*, no. 1 (Winter 1975): 16.

22 William W. Klein, Craig L. Blomberg, and Robert L. Hubbard Jr., *Introduction to Biblical Interpretation* (Grand Rapids, MI: Zondervan, 2017), 216.

sistent with either the immediate context of the Sermon on the Mount, or the broader message of the Bible as a whole, taking both the Hebrew and Greek Testaments into account. It is my belief, substantiated by the proofs I will lay before you in the coming chapters, that only a pronomian, constructive interpretation of πληρόω (*pleroo*) is tenable in light of the immediate context of the Sermon on the Mount and the broader witness of Scripture.

How Far Will This Book Go?

To establish strong proof for the resolution of the proper interpretation for Matthew 5:17, this book will focus on a very specific and delimited area of study. Though this in and of itself makes any conclusion we might draw easier to prove, the following chapters begin with specific, defined assumptions. This will make your task as the reader more manageable, and ensure that presuppositional matters that have been adequately addressed by other scholars will not hinder the thorough discussion of more central matters.

Limitations of Scope

As previously mentioned, this book only intends to extract what πληρόω (*pleroo*) meant in the mind of Jesus Christ. As such, the appearances of the word in broader Greek literature, uses from the Gospels where the speaker is not Jesus, and uses in the other books of the Apostolic Writings fall outside the primary focus of this study. While these other documents and passages make for interesting and useful study, they have also been studied in greater detail by previous scholars. As such, while examples of πληρόω (*pleroo*) from outside the discourses of Yeshua will be addressed for the sake of thoroughness, the treatment of these will not be as extensive as the treatment of πληρόω (*pleroo*) as used by Jesus in the Gospels.

Further, this book will primarily attempt to make a broad categorization of the meaning of πληρόω (*pleroo*) as it appears in Matthew 5:17, listing each form as destructive, constructive, or hybrid. It will aim to contribute material that is helpful for constructing a more precise definition of πληρόω (*pleroo*) and attendant model of the fulfillment of the Torah in Christ, but will not provide an exhaustive answer for either subject. Instead, the focus will always remain on answering the question of the broad categorization of meaning into which πληρόω (*pleroo*) may fall, guiding you to a range of interpretive options that fit this broad categorization.

Research Assumptions

Several key assumptions will also guide the research in this book. The most basic assumption in this regard is the historicity, accuracy, and general harmony of the accounts of Yeshua across the Gospels of Matthew, Mark, Luke, and John. Since this book presents a detailed analysis of the words spoken by Yeshua and reported by the Gospel writers, it is necessary to assume as a prerequisite that the words of Jesus as recorded in the Gospels were genuinely spoken by Yeshua, not added by a later redactor.

It is also necessary to assume that the statements of Yeshua as recorded in the Gospels accurately preserve at least the voice of Yeshua, if not His exact words. This assumption is necessary because the conclusions of the research in this book are dependent on the nuance of a single word as it appears in statements made by Yeshua. While the speculation of scholars that the Sermon on the Mount and other monologues of Yeshua could have originally transpired in Aramaic or even Hebrew is an interesting and provocative subject, it will only be given enough treatment here to show that, at least in the case of the word πληρόω (*pleroo*) specifically, if the Gospel writers were translating Jesus' words then their translations likely did not alter Jesus' meaning in a relevant or significant way.[23]

---

23 An example of a scholar who proposes that the Sermon on the Mount was originally delivered by Jesus in Hebrew is Brad H. Young, *Jesus the Jewish Theologian* (Grand Rapids, MI: Baker Academic, 1995), 185.

Chapter 1

What's Been Said Before

To cover any new ground with respect to understanding the meaning of πληρόω (*pleroo*) in Matthew 5:17, it is first necessary to assess the work of others who have gone before in researching this topic. Further, any relevant Biblical passages must be identified and compared with the opinions of these scholars. In this way, a foundation for the research of this book can be established that will help with the construction of a good rationale and argument for the conclusion.

Biblical Overview

As might be expected, the central passage around which the research will revolve is Matthew 5:17. In the Greek text of the NA28 Edition of the Greek New Testament, the verse reads, "Μὴ νομίσητε ὅτι ἦλθον καταλῦσαι τὸν νόμον ἢ τοὺς προφήτας· οὐκ ἦλθον καταλῦσαι ἀλλὰ πληρῶσαι." (In transliteration: *Me nomisete hoti elthon katalusai ton nomon he tous prophetas; ouk elthon katalusai alla plerosai.*) No variants are noted in the Nestle-Aland apparatus (notes on manuscript variants), which is strong grounds to surmise that this reading is original beyond reasonable doubt.[1]

Although this text is central to the conclusion of the research, its final interpretation is heavily dependent on the analysis of other relevant passages, and as such, its analysis will be postponed until Chapter 4. According to the limitations set previously, the most relevant Scriptures are the verses from the Gospels that use πληρόω (*pleroo*) in the speech of Yeshua. There are nineteen verses, not counting Matthew 5:17 itself, that fit these limitations. While this is not a large number, it is enough

1 Barbara Aland et al., eds., *Novum Testamentum Graece 28th Edition* (Munster, Germany: Deutsche Bibelgesellschaft, 2012), 10.

to derive useful information about the meaning of πληρόω (*pleroo*) in Matthew 5:17. An assessment of each of these individual verses will be conducted in Chapter 3.

πληρόω as Defined by Lexica

Although the primary focus is on πληρόω (*pleroo*) as used by Yeshua, it is still important to consider its broader meaning, as this will establish the general semantic range of πληρόω (*pleroo*) and reveal possible ways Yeshua could have used the word. To identify this semantic range, primary lexica (dictionaries) will be consulted for their definitions. These definitions will then be tested in the Septuagint,[2] the Apostolic Writings (New Testament), and extrabiblical Greek literature to confirm or challenge them and to observe the degree to which each definition may be regarded as a regular or irregular use of πληρόω (*pleroo*).

BDAG offers six glosses[3] of πληρόω (*pleroo*) to capture its semantic range.[4] The first and most frequently used definition is the concrete meaning of the verb, "to make full." The term can be used hyperbolically, conceptually, and metaphorically. The alternate definitions include "complete a period of time," "bring to completion that which was already begun," "bring to a designed end," "bring to completion an activity in which one has been involved from its beginning," and "complete a number."[5] The *Cambridge Greek Lexicon* and BrillDAG confirm the basic concrete meaning of "fill" or "to fill up"[6] with slight abstractions includ-

---

2 The Septiagint (abbreviated LXX) is an ancient translation of the Old Testament from Hebrew into Greek.

3 A *gloss* is a suggested word for use in translation.

4 *Semantic range* refers to the range of possible meanings for a word. For example, romance can mean love in the context of marriage or courtship or it can mean "coming from Latin" as in the sentence "Spanish is a Romance language." Both these uses are parts of the semantic range of the word "romance."

5 BDAG, s.v. "πληρόω," 1:828.

6 Franco Montanari et al., s.v. "πληρόω," BrillDAG, 1:1685.

ing "satisfy," "empanel," "fit out," "supply," and "render in full."[7] More abstract uses include "complete a period of time" and "traverse."[8]

According to Louw & Nida, the active forms of πληρόω (*pleroo*) occur in seven semantic domains. These are most relevant because Matthew 5:17 uses an active form of πληρόω (*pleroo*). In its most basic form, πληρόω (*pleroo*) means "to cause something to become full."[9] It alternately can refer to the completion of a tally,[10] the finishing of all steps in an activity,[11] a completeness of provision,[12] the full relation of a message,[13] the true meaning of something,[14] and it can take a causative sense.[15]

This survey helps provide a general overview of the semantic range of πληρόω (*pleroo*), but sometimes the long lists of glosses and definitions can make it challenging to see the connections between the various meanings of a word. In the case of πληρόω (*pleroo*), the basic meaning of the verb is best understood by way of a spatial analogy, that of filling a container up to capacity. This is the concrete referent of πληρόω (*pleroo*), and the remainder of its semantic range consists of metaphorical abstractions from the concrete spatial meaning, a fact observable both in the range of Louw & Nida definitions,[16] as well as in Silva's comments on the word group in the *New International Dictionary of New Testament Theology and Exegesis*.[17] Having established this, the meaning of πληρόω

7 James Diggle et al., s.v. "πληρόω," *The Cambridge Greek Lexicon* 1:1143.
8 Diggle et al. s.v. "πληρόω," *The Cambridge Greek Lexicon* 1:1143.
9 Johannes P. Louw and Eugene A. Nida, s.v. "πληρόωa," L&N, 59.37.
10 L&N, s.v., "πληρόω[b], ἀναπληρόω[a]," 59.33.
11 L&N, s.v., "πληρόω[c]," 68.26.
12 L&N, s.v., "πληρόω[d]," 35.33.
13 L&N, s.v., "πληρόω[e], πληροφορέω[b]," 33.199.
14 L&N, s.v., "πληρόω[f]," 33.144.
15 L&N, s.v., "πληροφορέω[a], πληρόω[g], ἐκπληρόω, ἀναπληρόω[c], πίμπλημι[b]," 13.106.
16 L&N, s.v., "πληρόω," 13.106, 33.144, 33.199, 35.33, 59.33, 68.26.
17 Moises Silva, "πληρόω," NIDNTTE, G4444:JL 2.

(*pleroo*) must now be refined by assessment of actual uses of πληρόω (*pleroo*) in various ancient sources.

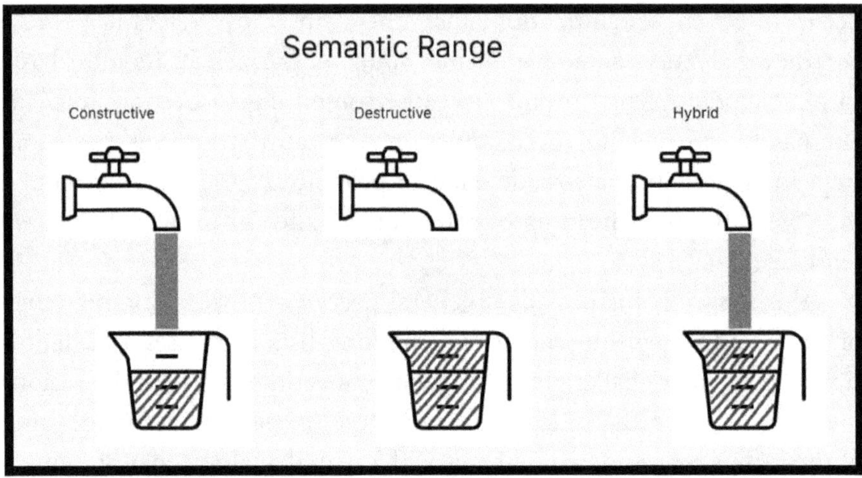

Figure 1: The semantic range of πληρόω (*pleroo*) as it relates to its constructive, destructive, and hybrid uses.

- The constructive meaning for πληρόω (*pleroo*) focuses on the process of filling, the water running into the cup.
- The destructive meaning focuses on the result, the fact that the cup is full.
- The hybrid part has some degree of focus on both the process and result, viewing the act of filling the cup as a totality from start to finish. Hybrid uses of πληρόω (*pleroo*) can have varying degrees of emphasis, sometimes more on the process (constructive) and sometimes more on the result (destructive) aspect.

πληρόω in the Septuagint

The Septuagint, an ancient translation of the Tanach into the Greek language, frequently uses πληρόω (*pleroo*) to translate the Hebrew מלא

(pronounced and transliterated *mala*),[18] a verb that corresponds closely to the meaning of πληρόω (*pleroo*) in its connotations of "fill up" and "carry out."[19] In these uses, the meaning of πληρόω (*pleroo*) is frequently revealed by the recipient of the verbal action.[20] In Genesis 1:22, the direct object of the πληρόω (*pleroo*) form is τὰ ὕδατα (transliterated *ta hudata*), "the waters." Because this recipient of the verbal action is tangible and impersonal, this use of πληρόω (*pleroo*) is in accordance with its concrete meaning, translated "fill the waters." Another literal but more idiomatic meaning is in Exodus 32:29, where πληρόω (*pleroo*) is part of a phrase that woodenly translates the Hebrew מִלְאוּ יֶדְכֶם (transliterated *miloo yed'chem*). While the direct object is tangible, the phrase represents a use that lies outside the normal range for πληρόω (*pleroo*), a use often rendered by the English word "consecrate" (Exodus 32:29 NASB95.)[21] An abstract use of πληρόω (*pleroo*) on the other hand is 1 Kings 7:2, where the Indirect Object of the πληρόω form is τῆς τέχνης (transliterated *tes technes*), "skill" (LXX Rahlf's). Because the Indirect Object is intangible, the πληρόω (*pleroo*) form refers to an abstract meaning, that Hiram possessed great construction skills. This abstract use often refers to emotions, especially the emotional seizure of a person with fear, grief, joy, etc.[22]

---

18 Delling Gerhard, "πληρόω," *TNDT* 1:868.

19 HALOT, s.v. "מלא," p. 1:583.

20 The *recipient of the verbal action* is a term coined by the author. The recipient of the verbal action differs in grammatical case and function within the clause or sentence in which it appears depending on the form of its verb. For active verbal forms, the recipient of the verbal action is the Direct Object, and if present the Indirect Object. For passive verbal forms, the recipient of the verbal action is the Subject. In all cases however, the recipient or recipients of the verbal action is/are directly affected by the action of the verbal form to which it is/they are connected.

21 *TNDT*, 1:868.

22 BDAG, s.v., "πληρόω," 1:828.

These examples may be considered constructive in that they primarily communicate an additive sense. πληρόω (*pleroo*) is used destructively, however, and one such use is Numbers 6:5, where the direct object is αἱ ἡμέραι (transliterated *ai hemerai*), "the days," and in this use the πληρόω (*pleroo*) form refers to the close of a specified time. Regardless of the amount of time specified, when the recipient of the verbal action of πληρόω (*pleroo*) is related to time, the verb always refers to the closure of a time period.[23] Two other uses of πληρόω (*pleroo*) in the LXX involve a sense of closure, where prayer or prophecy is the direct object, as in 2 Chronicles 26:21. In both situations πληρόω (*pleroo*) carries a sense of "bring about" and refers to the act of causing the answer to the prayer, or the event foreseen by the prophecy, to happen.[24] That said, these uses are not purely constructive, for they involve a sense of closure, but are not purely destructive either, for they also involve the additive idea of realization. As such, these instances are a hybrid use of πληρόω (*pleroo*) featuring both constructive and destructive elements.

The preceding examples and uses of πληρόω (*pleroo*) are further illuminated by the definitions listed in *A Greek-English Lexicon of the Septuagint* (*GELS*), which lists nine definitions for πληρόω (*pleroo*). Not surprisingly, the first definition is the basic connotation of the word, the meaning "to fill."[25] Other definitions, such as "to complete a period of time" and "to bring to completion" corroborate the definitions fielded by other lexica, however, some of the definitions in *GELS* are more unique.[26] Specifically, the definition "to consecrate" covers the specialized uses where πληρόω (*pleroo*) translates formulaic uses of מלא (*mala*) as in Exod 32:29, the definition "multiply" cited by *GELS* as occurring in Psalm 109:6, and the definition "to bring the end of the life and existence of"

23 BDAG, s.v., "πληρόω," 1:828.

24 *TNDT*, 1:868.

25 *GELS*, s.v., "πληρόω," 1:565.

26 *GELS*, s.v., "πληρόω," 1:565.

in Daniel 5:26.[27] These uses are not readily attested by other lexica or by sources outside the Septuagint, so it appears that these uses are specialized and largely unique to the Septuagint's use of πληρόω (*pleroo*).

The frequent use of πληρόω (*pleroo*) to translate forms of מלא (*mala*) has led some scholars to postulate that the Sermon on the Mount as preserved in the Gospels is a Greek translation from an original sermon delivered in Hebrew or Aramaic, and that the form of πληρόω (*pleroo*) found in Matthew 5:17 translates an original Hebrew מלא (*mala*).[28] If the postulation that the Sermon on the Mount was originally delivered in a Semitic language is accepted, the similar semantic range of מלא and its Aramaic equivalent to πληρόω (*pleroo*) suggests that the conclusion of these scholars regarding the original Hebrew or Aramaic wording is very likely.[29]

In his commentary on Matthew, pronomian scholar Tim Hegg favors the idea that the Sermon on the Mount was originally spoken in Hebrew. Hegg uses the verses of Jeremiah 44:25 and 1 Kings 1:13–14 to show that a meaning of "establish" or "confirm" is an attested use for both מלא (*mala*), which is used in the Masoretic Text of these verses, and πληρόω (*pleroo*), which is found in the LXX text as the translation for מלא (*mala*) in both instances.[30] Interestingly, the oldest Hebrew translations of Matthew use מלא (*mala*) to translate πληρόω (*pleroo*), strengthening the notion that the semantic range of these words have strong overlap.[31]

While at first glance the interpretation of πληρόω (*pleroo*) based on מלא (*mala*) appears to have many strengths, it is simply not certain that

---

27 *GELS*, s.v., "πληρόω," 1:565.

28 Marc A. Clausen, "An Exegetical and Theological Examination of Matthew 5:17-20", (Thes., Liberty University, 1993), 67–68. Scholars Crossing.

29 Hayim ben Yosef Tawil, s.v. "מלא," *Akkadian Lexical Companion for Biblical Hebrew Etymological, Semantic and Idiomatic Equivalence with Supplement on Biblical Aramaic* (New York: Ktav, 2009), 1:212.

30 Tim Hegg, *Commentary on the Gospel of Matthew: Volume 1* (Tacoma, WA: TorahResource, 2007), 174.

31 Hegg, *Matthew*, 173.

the Sermon on the Mount was spoken in Hebrew or Aramaic and then translated by Matthew into Greek. It is still possible that the Sermon was originally spoken in Greek, for the use of this language would have permitted the broadest possible audience to understand the meaning of the sermon.[32] Further, although Hegg does prove "establish, confirm" as an attested use for מלא (*mala*) and πληρόω (*pleroo*), the fact that he only cites two uses with this meaning seems to indicate that this use is at least rare for πληρόω (*pleroo*) if not מלא (*mala*). For these two reasons, and because the semantic ranges of מלא (*mala*) and πληρόω (*pleroo*) are so similar, it is unlikely that studying possible Hebrew and Aramaic equivalents for πληρόω (*pleroo*) in Matthew 5:17 will provide more than a few additional possiblilities. However, any meaning assigned from an equivalent Semitic word is based on a postulation that simply cannot be confirmed or denied due to lack of evidence. As such, these possible meanings have weak support at best.

πληρόω in the New Testament

In the Gospels of Matthew and John, πληρόω (*pleroo*) is used frequently in reference to prophecies from the Tanach, especially in Matthew, where twelve of the sixteen appearances of πληρόω (*pleroo*) in the book feature this use.[33] Some conclude from this that the meaning of πληρόω (*pleroo*) as used by Matthew carries a hybrid meaning in all cases.[34] Others note that all twelve references to prophecy use a Passive form of πληρόω

32 Quarles notes that some grammatical features of the Beatitudes suggest an original Greek composition. See Charles L. Quarles, *Matthew*, EGGNT (Nashville, TN: B&H Academic, 2017), 46.

33 Bradley M. Trout, "Matthew 5:17 and Matthew's Community" *HTS* 72, no. 3 (2016): 3.

34 Trout, "Community," 5.

(*pleroo*), and all NT references to fulfilled prophecy use the Passive except Acts 3:18 (NA28) and 13:27.[35]

Aside from its use to mark references to the Tanach, πληρόω (*pleroo*) often denotes a person or group being filled with emotions, traits, or even the Holy Spirit, as in Acts 13:52.[36] In Acts 5:28, the term refers to the proliferation of Christian teaching in Jerusalem. Literal uses are attested as well, including Matthew 13:48.[37] Several times, πληρόω (*pleroo*) refers to the passage of time, including Acts 7:23. In Revelation 6:11, it refers to completion of a numerical tally, and it is also used to express one's needs being met, as in Philippians 4:18.

These uses generally corroborate the definitions fielded by BDAG and Louw and Nida, but the definition listed in Louw and Nida as πληρόω[f] is suspect. The definition as listed is "to give the true or complete meaning to something," implying a corrective or completive sense.[38] Matthew 5:17 and Galatians 5:14 are listed as examples, but Galatians 5:14 does not require a corrective sense,[39] and the use in Matthew 5:17 is likewise debated, as has been shown. Given that both passages are the subject of dispute, it is likely that πληρόω[f] is an erroneous definition.

Other Relevant Passages

One additional group of relevant Biblical passages are those which reveal principles regarding the relationship between the Christian and the Torah, though these passages may not use πληρόω (*pleroo*). A primary text in this regard is John 1:17, which in the King James Version appears to

---

35 Hegg, *Matthew*, 173.

36 Eldon Woodcock, "The Filling of the Holy Spirit," BibSac 157, no. 1 (January-March 2000): 68.

37 Woodcock, "Filling," 69.

38 *L&N*, s.v., "πληρόωf," 33.144.

39 Thomas R. Schreiner, *Galatians*, ECNT (Grand Rapids, MI: Zondervan Academic, 2010), 335.

support the notion that the Torah and Christ are at odds, suggesting that believers in the era before the coming of Yeshua were saved by keeping the Law, whereas believers from the time of Christ forward are saved by grace.[40] However, many note that other verses in the Apostolic Scriptures contradict this reading of the verse, including Galatians 3:6–7.[41]

Scholars of both the antinomian and pronomian camps acknowledge that the Apostolic Writings make statements that view the Torah in a positive light.[42] Romans 7 enumerates the Torah's virtues in that it is not sin (Romans 7:7 NASB95), is holy, righteous, good, spiritual (Romans 7:12-14), and is "the law of God" (Romans 7:22). Further, scholars of both perspectives agree that the Torah is not a means of achieving salvation, as shown in Galatians 5:3 and James 2:10. Rather, the Torah presents God's standard for righteous living (Romans 7:25) and reveals the sinful condition of humanity.[43] The question this leaves unanswered then is not one of whether the Torah is spiritually relevant for believers, but of whether it is practically relevant, whether the Torah represents a Law that the Christian should fully obey inasmuch as he or she is able. While many antinomians and pronomians agree that the work of Christ did not change the substance of the Torah, where these two general schools of thought disagree most sharply is over whether the work of Christ brought about changes to the mode of the Torah's administration and its application to the lives of believers.[44]

---

40 John Henry Bernard, St. *John: Volume 1:1–7* (London: Bloomsbury T&T Clark, 1999), 29.

41 Millard J. Erickson, *Christian Theology: Third Edition* (Grand Rapids, MI: Baker Academic, 2013), 906.

42 Erickson, *Christian Theology*, 907.

43 Erickson, *Christian Theology*, 734.

44 Du Toit, "Dialectical Approach," 59.

Survey of Scholarly Opinions: Church Fathers

The issue of the Torah as it relates to Christians was recognized in the earliest centuries of the Church. However, with respect to Matthew 5:17, it is instructive to note that while the Church Fathers do cite or allude to this verse in constructing their views on the Torah's relationship to Christians, they generally treat the meaning of πληρόω (*pleroo*) as self-evident and without need for clarification. Thus, any conclusions on the meaning of πληρόω (*pleroo*) in the minds of the Fathers must be inferred from their broader views on the relationship of Christ to the Torah.

The majority view of the Church Fathers is perhaps expressed most succinctly by Epiphanius, who, in condemning the pronomian views of the Nazarene sect, writes: "It is clear to all who have any intelligence whatever that Christ came that the Law might be fulfilled; he [sic] did not come destroying the Law but rather fulfilling it, and he [sic] determined to take away the curse which resulted from transgressing the Law."[45] This quote from Epiphanius shows that he assigns a meaning of "obey, keep" to πληρόω (*pleroo*), and that Christ's perfect obedience to the Law brought about major changes to the way the Law applies to Christians. From Epiphanius and Augustine onward, the Fathers speak with a unified voice that to keep the Law is sinful and that so doing amounts to clinging to an outmoded form of worship to God.[46]

Augustine wrote in *On Christian Doctrine* that the fulfillment of the Law by the Christian constitutes love, calling to mind Jesus' statements in Matthew 22:37–40.[47] Further, in his commentary on the Sermon on the Mount, Augustine expressly comments on the meaning of πληρόω

---

45 Epiphanius, *Against All Heresies*, 29.8.2, in Ray A. Pritz, *Nazarene Jewish Christianity: From the End of the New Testament Period Until Its Disappearance in the Fourth Century* (Jerusalem: Magnes Press, 1988), 30–35.

46 Ray A. Pritz, *Nazarene Jewish Christianity: From the End of the New Testament Period Until Its Disappearance in the Fourth Century* (Jerusalem: Magnes Press, 1988), 76.

47 Augustine, *On Christian Doctrine*, 1.35.39 (NPNF 1.2).

(*pleroo*), positing that the word has a double meaning: it refers both to Messiah's obedience to the Law and to His addition of what the Law lacked.[48] Thus, it may be deduced that in the view of the later Fathers, the weighty matters of the Torah such as love apply to the Christian, but it is a mistake to think that the literal keeping of the whole of Torah is necessary for believers. Eventually, this view of Torah even came to be found implicitly within the terms "Old Testament" and "New Testament," which distinguish the Scriptures considered by the Fathers to be fully relevant for Christians from the Scriptures considered to be less relevant.[49]

In the early centuries, however, especially the second, there is evidence of competing views among the Fathers on the relevance of the Torah for Christians. On the one side, Ignatius in his *Letter to the Magnesians* unequivocally supports the later majority view that the Law is not for Christians to keep as written.[50] On the other side, late first and early second century writings such as *1 Clement* and *The Shepherd of Hermas* paint a more positive portrait of the Law as lived out by Christians.[51] Eusebius also documents disputes on issues related to Law observance which took place during the second century, specifically regarding the calculation of the day of Easter.[52] Bishop Victor of Rome took the antinomian view and argued that Easter should always be a Sunday, while Bishop Polycrates of Ephesus defended the pronomian idea of celebrating it on the 14th of Nissan.[53]

---

48 Augustine, *Our Lord's Sermon on the Mount*, 1.8.20 (NPNF 6.1).

49 See *Collected Letters of Saint Basil*, letter 232.

50 Ignatius, *To the Magnesians*, 10.3.

51 See 1 Clement 1:3, 2:7-8, 3:4, 7:2, 10:1-2, 13:3-4, 15:1-4, 27:2, 40:1-2, 43:1, 49:1, 50:4, 58:2, and Herm. Vis. 7.3.4 (2.3).

52 Eusebius, *Ecclesiastical History*, 5.23.1. Note that Greek does not have a separate word to distinguish the Biblical "Passover" from the modern "Easter," so I am using these terms interchangeably in the discussion about Eusebius.

53 Eusebius, *Ecclesiastical History*, 5.23.1.

There is very strong evidence to suggest that until the third century or so, the issue of whether a Christian should observe the Mosaic Law was considered a non-salvific matter of disagreement among various churches. In the dispute over the day of Easter mentioned previously, Bishop Irenaeus of Lyon brokered peace between Victor and Polycrates by observing that from the early second century, in the time of Bishop Sixtus of Rome, the bishops of Rome had kept a Sunday Easter but maintained peace with those Christians who honored Jesus's resurrection on Passover.[54] In like manner, Justin Martyr in the mid-second century wrote that it was acceptable in his view for a Christian to keep the Law, although he himself did not do so.[55] The first instance where a group is regarded as heretical specifically because of their observance of the Law is in the fourth-century writings of Epiphanius, in his condemnation of the Nazarene sect.[56]

Based on these facts, it appears that the dispute between pronomian and antinomian views of the Law is extremely early, with a likely origin in the early second century. This implies that both views on Matthew 5:17 trace back at least to this time as well, and that both views were considered orthodox until the late third or early fourth century, at which time the pronomian view came to be regarded as heretical. Because of the duration of the dispute, and the fact that it was not considered a salvation issue in the early centuries, it is difficult to establish which viewpoint was the perspective of Christ and the Apostles based on early Christian literature alone. However, Dr. Benjamin Szumskyj notes in his doctoral dissertation that the earliest documents with hints of support

54 Eusebius, *Ecclesiastical History*, 5.24.14.

55 Justin Martyr, *Dialogue with Trypho the Jew*, 46.1 (PG 6.573).

56 Epiphanius, *Against All Heresies*, 29.7, in Ray A. Pritz, *Nazarene Jewish Christianity: From the End of the New Testament Period Until Its Disappearance in the Fourth Century* (Jerusalem: Magnes Press, 1988), 30–35.

for a pronomian view date to the late first century, which makes this view plausibly extant during the lifetime of the last surviving Apostles.[57]

Survey of Scholarly Opinions: Modern Scholars

The debate concerning the mode of the Law's administration is a direct outgrowth of the study of Christ's relationship to the Law. Consequently, the definition chosen for πληρόω (*pleroo*) in Matthew 5:17 often determines the side of the debate on which a particular scholar falls. Those who adopt a destructive or hybrid definition typically articulate an antinomian perspective, and those who assign a constructive meaning commonly express a pronomian view. This can be shown by assessing several key sources that reflect variations within each perspective, which will reveal both the points of unity shared by each school of thought and the intellectual diversity present within them.

An excellent example of a modern antinomian perspective of Christ's relationship to the Law may be found in Craig L. Blomberg's commentary on the Gospel of Matthew. Successfully avoiding the problems associated with creating oversimplified rules of thumb concerning the Law's relevance for the believer, Blomberg argues that in fulfilling the Law, Christ was bringing it to its intended goal, neither contradicting the Law nor leaving it unaltered.[58] Blomberg acknowledges that Matthew 5:17 is a challenge to both the classic Reformed and the Dispensationalist views of the Law, and even manages to find common ground with more pronomian positions over and against antinomian perspectives when he notes that "It is inadequate to say either that none of the Old Testament applies unless it is explicitly reaffirmed in the New or that all of the Old Testa-

---

57 Benjamin John Stephan Szumskyj, "The Role of the Law in the Sanctification of the Believer Today: A Brief Introduction to Pronomianism" Doctoral Dissertation, Liberty University, 2024, 30.

58 Craig L. Blomberg, *Matthew: An Exegetical and Theological Exposition of Holy Scripture*, NAC (Nashville, TN: B&H Academic, 1992), 90.

ment applies unless it is explicitly revoked in the New. Rather, all of the Old Testament remains normative and relevant for Jesus' followers…"[59] The next part of his sentence, however, is decidedly more antinomian in outlook: "…But none of it can be rightly interpreted until one understands how it has been fulfilled in Christ."[60] In this respect, Blomberg's hybrid interpretation of πληρόω (*pleroo*) forms a key pillar in support of his view that Christ brought about changes to the Law.

Another modern perspective on πληρόω (*pleroo*) in Matthew 5:17 comes from Zulkifli Oddeng, who writes in his article "Pleromacy: When Jesus Interpreted the Law and the Prophets" that Jesus' purpose in "fulfilling" the law was to affirm the Law while giving it a new meaning.[61] In other words, Oddeng maintains that Jesus fulfilled the Law by giving His Divinely Inspired interpretation of the same, a thoroughly hybrid understanding of πληρόω (*pleroo*). To support this notion Oddeng depends on the broader context of the Sermon on the Mount and specifically the "You have heard it said… but I say to you…" series of statements that follow Matthew 5:17 in the discourse.[62]

A more antinomian perspective may be observed in the work of W.D. Davies and Dale C. Allison Jr., who in their commentary on Matthew lay out many interpretive options for πληρόω (*pleroo*), including both constructive and destructive options, before concluding that, in their view, the best understanding combines elements of transcendence and eschatological fulfillment.[63] Their theory of transcendence is based on the context of Matthew 5:21–48, where Davies and Allison understand Jesus to add additional demands to those imposed by the Mosaic Law.

---

59 Blomberg, *Matthew*, 90.

60 Blomberg, *Matthew*, 90.

61 Zulkifli Oddeng, "Pleromacy: When Jesus Interpreted the Law and the Prophets" *Studium Biblicum* 1, no. 1 (2024): 52–53.

62 Oddeng, "Pleromacy," 53.

63 W.D. Davies and Dale C. Allison Jr., *A Critical and Exegetical Commentary on the Gospel According to Saint Matthew: Introduction and Commentary on Matthew I-VII, Volume I*, ICC (Edinburgh: T&T Clark, 1988), 486.

Based on this, they conclude that Jesus viewed Himself as transcending the Mosaic Law, with the right to change and re-shape that Law as He wished.[64] Davies and Allison note that Jesus' citation is not just of the Law, but of "The Law or the Prophets" (Matthew 5:17), which they understand as giving Jesus' statement a prophetic and thus eschatological import, pointing to the fulfillment of the Scriptures in both the first and second comings of Christ.[65]

A more traditional antinomian perspective is held by the author of the Matthew section of a 1906 Bible commentary, which articulates the view of Christ's supersession of the Law that was later reformulated as part of Davies' and Allison's view. While the commentator states that "In one respect Christ's attitude to the Law was conservative...He could even repeat the current teaching of the rabbis that the Law was eternal...,"[66] he adds to this idea that Christ's view was that the Law's eternal validity was not in itself, but as "...Developed, or completed by Christ."[67] In this way, the commentator is able to argue that the Law remains spiritually valid to Christians as a type and shadow of the work of Christ, but that the work of Christ changed entirely the mode and substance of the Law's practical significance. In this respect, the commentator lists several specific commands of the OT Law:

> The Law of Sacrifice was fulfilled in His sacrificial death, and in the spiritual sacrifices of prayer and praise... Circumcision became 'the circumcision made without hands,' i.e. Holy Baptism. The Passover became the Lord's Supper. The sanctification which the Law gave to one day in seven, was extended by Christ to every day in the week, and even the sabbath itself was, in a certain sense, perpetuated and continued by Him as the

64 Davies and Allison, *Saint Matthew*, 486.

65 Davies and Allison, *Saint Matthew*, 486.

66 Dummeflow, *Commentary*, 641.

67 Dummeflow, *Commentary*, 641.

> Christian 'Lord's Day.' Even such minor matters as ceremonial ablutions and the distinction of meats received their due fulfillment when Christ made possible the inward holiness which these outward observances symbolised.[68]

In particular, the last sentence makes this commentator's perspective on the meaning of πληρόω (*pleroo*) clear, giving it a practical meaning equivalent to "supersede, abolish, or replace." While this perspective sees the Torah as a spiritual foreshadow of Christ, the need for its practical observance has ceased on account of the work of Christ, who produced a new Law that is to guide the Christian life in place of the commandments laid out in the Torah. To cite Blomberg, it appears that this perspective affirms that "…None of the Old Testament applies unless it is explicitly reaffirmed in the New…," at least in the practical sense of the word *apply*.[69]

Arren Bennet Lawrence, in his response to the position of Richard E. Menninger, notes several weaknesses with the traditional antinomian position that the Law in whole is superseded by Christ, especially that the Old Testament never anticipates such an event, and that the traditional antinomian position has difficulty explaining how the transcendence or replacement of the Law is distinct from the destruction of the Law that Jesus expressly says He has not come to do.[70] On this account, Lawrence proceeds to give his own analysis of πληρόω (*pleroo*) and concludes that the best understanding of this verb is constructive and pronomian, referring to Jesus' affirmation of and obedience to the Law. For Lawrence,

---

68 Dummeflow, *Commentary*, 641.

69 Blomberg, *Matthew*, 90.

70 Arren Bennet Lawrence, *Comparative Characterization in the Sermon on the Mount: Characterization of the Ideal Disciple* (Eugene, OR: Wipf & Stock, 2017), 110.

"We see Jesus teaching his [sic] disciples that he [sic] did not come to destroy the Law but to obey and to affirm its validity and existence."[71]

Another scholar who articulates a more pronomian view of πληρόω (*pleroo*) and Matthew 5:17 is Willoughby C. Allen, who briefly comments, "Christ did not come to overthrow the Mosaic law, which was to be eternally binding upon the hearts and consciences of men… Commentators have exhausted their ingenuity in attempts to explain away this passage, but its meaning is too clear to be misunderstood."[72] Although in this one case Allen adopts a pronomian interpretation, his personally formulated theology of the relationship between Christ and the Law is antinomian because Allen argues that Matthew 5:17 is an editorial gloss.[73] Thus, Allen's work represents a fusion of the antinomian and pronomian perspectives, which depends on the assumption of a heavily edited Gospel text, an assumption which leads Allen to argue that Matthew 5:17 is a pronomian verse inserted into the antinomian Sermon on the Mount.[74]

Another pronomian perspective is given by Gregory McKenzie, who addresses Matthew 5:17 at multiple places in his dissertation, "Pronomian Paradigm: A pro-Torah, Christocentric Method of Theology and Apologetics." While he does not directly comment on the definition of πληρόω (*pleroo*), he does indirectly argue for a constructive definition of the term by noting the contrastive structure of the discourse within Matthew 5:17, and on the grounds of this contrastive structure makes the case that to interpret πληρόω (*pleroo*) in a destructive manner would cause the verse to be self-contradictory in practice if not in its literal wording.[75] Instead, McKenzie argues that the broader teachings of Jesus

---

71 Lawrence, *Comparative Characterization*, 117.

72 Willoughby C. Allen, *St. Matthew* (London: T&T Clark International, 2004), 45.

73 Allen, *St. Matthew*, 45.

74 Allen, *St. Matthew*, 45.

75 Gregory Scott McKenzie, "Pronomian Paradigm: A Pro-Torah, Christocentric Method of Theology and Apologetics" (2024): *Doctoral Dissertations and Projects*, 5623, 61. https://digitalcommons.liberty.edu/doctoral/5623.

and the NT confirm a constructive interpretation of πληρόω (*pleroo*), stating, "In this case, [on the road to Emmaus] Christ simply explained (Lk. 24:32) how the Law and Prophets pointed to him [sic]... if one simply takes Christ at his [sic] word... Christ in Mt. 5:17-20 confirms non-abolition."[76]

Identifying Helpful Contexts

As discussed in the Introduction, the interpretation of Matthew 5:17 is largely a debate between two major theoretical frameworks, which are the antinomian and pronomian perspectives with their corresponding destructive and constructive interpretations of πληρόω (*pleroo*). However, one key factor with the ability to determine a given researcher's conclusion regarding the meaning of πληρόω (*pleroo*) is which other uses of this word are seen as the closest corresponding contexts to the example in Matthew 5:17. As shown in the Biblical Overview section, πληρόω (*pleroo*) is used in many different contexts in the Bible with several different attendant meanings, though most of those meanings are a greater or lesser abstraction from the concrete referent of πληρόω (*pleroo*). To uncover the uses of πληρόω (*pleroo*) within Ancient Greek Literature as a whole that are most similar to how the word is used in Matthew 5:17, the first step is to survey uses of πληρόω (*pleroo*) in literature from outside the Bible, including that of the early Church. This will show an array of options on which uses of πληρόω (*pleroo*) establish the best framework for uncovering its meaning as used in Matthew 5:17, which can then be sifted through to discover the best criteria for calling a particular use of πληρόω (*pleroo*) similar or dissimilar to the use in Matthew 5:17.

76 McKenzie, "Pronomian Paradigm," 60.

πληρόω as Used in Ancient Greek Literature

In addition to the Biblical uses of πληρόω (*pleroo*) previously discussed, forms of this verb appear frequently in ancient Greek texts. Of particular relevance to its use in Matthew 5:17 are those texts that use the same verbal form as is used in that verse: the aorist active infinitive πληρῶσαι (*plerosai*). When assessing the uses of this word in ancient Greek literature, although there is variance in its use, some trends are apparent.[77] Approximately four out of every five uses carry a constructive meaning, and these are about evenly split between concrete uses and more abstract ones. There are only a few referents for which πληρῶσαι (*plerosai*) is used destructively, including the completion of an act,[78] the satisfaction of one's desires or nature,[79] the payment of a debt,[80] and, as in the Septuagint, the close of a period of time.[81]

The constructive uses of πληρῶσαι (*plerosai*) are varied and encompass both concrete and abstract uses of the term. Although the total number of occurrences is close to equal for concrete and abstract constructive uses of πληρῶσαι (*plerosai*), there is a distinct disparity between Christian and secular literature in these uses. While secular literature attests both concrete and abstract constructive uses, there is a decided bias toward concrete uses with these forming about two thirds of the constructive uses within secular literature. Christian literature is heavily weighted in the other direction with the great majority of constructive uses being abstract, with πληρῶσαι (*plerosai*) only being used in a concrete constructive manner one time within the Christian literature surveyed.[82]

---

77 The following analysis is based on my personal examination of the uses of πληρῶσαι within the documents of the Loeb Classical Library. Accessed February 3, 2025.

78 Eusebius, *Ecclesiastical History*, 1.13.10.

79 Josephus, *Jewish Antiquities*, 17.237.

80 *Select Papyri: Correspondence*, 434.28.

81 Galen, *Hygiene*, 6.387K.

82 Herm. Sim., 84.5 (9.7).

With these observations in mind, several conclusions may be drawn. Foremost, both in the Scriptures and in extrabiblical literature πληρόω (*pleroo*) is used with destructive meanings as well as constructive ones, placing both within the possible semantic range of πληρόω (*pleroo*) as it is used in Greek in general. While the term is used constructively with greater frequency, this does not prove that πληρόω (*pleroo*) is by nature constructive. Stronger evidence in this regard is that πληρόω (*pleroo*) is only used destructively with respect to a limited number of referents. As such, it is best to conclude that if a given use of πληρόω (*pleroo*) does not refer to one of these referents where the verb is frequently used destructively, it is likely that the use of πληρόω (*pleroo*) in question has some kind of constructive meaning. Finally, the anomalous heavy use of πληρῶσαι (*plerosai*) with an abstract constructive meaning in early Christian literature suggests that the term acquired a meaning in Christian circles which was somewhat distinct from the term's meaning as used in secular contexts. As such, uses of πληρόω (*pleroo*) in secular Greek literature may be less helpful for uncovering the meaning of the term as it was used by Christ.

Survey of Possible Contexts for Interpreting πληρόω in Matthew 5:17

As shown by the survey of secular Greek uses of πληρῶσαι (*plerosai*), believing that non-Christian and extrabiblical uses of πληρόω (*pleroo*) to be the best context for adjudicating the interpretation of Matthew 5:17 would be flawed due to the large margin by which concrete uses of the term are favored over abstract uses. Early Christian extrabiblical literature provides useful insight as to how the early Church understood the term, but because this literature likely post-dates the composition of the Gospel of Matthew and frequently uses πληρῶσαι (*plerosai*) as a word of Christian technical jargon, these uses provide only limited insight into the meaning Christ originally intended for πληρῶσαι (*plerosai*) in Matthew 5:17.[83]

Not surprisingly, scholarship has focused little attention on comparing Matthew 5:17 to extrabiblical writings, and it is a challenge to find any serious scholars who propose that the best context for interpreting Matthew 5:17 is found in extrabiblical literature. A more popular option within the scholarly community is to opine that the best context for interpreting Matthew 5:17 is the other uses of πληρόω (*pleroo*) throughout the book.[84] This leads scholars who adopt this approach to consider the fulfillment citations of Matthew as the most relevant uses for clarifying Matthew 5:17. As shown in the Biblical Overview, πληρόω (*pleroo*) is used the great majority of the time in Matthew's Gospel to introduce a quote or allusion to the Tanach. This approach best informs a scholarly approach to interpreting Matthew 5:17 in its foundational supposition, which is that the most relevant context for the resolution of a disputed definition is found within the body of works composed by the same author.[85]

Another possible approach compares πληρόω (*pleroo*) in Matthew 5:17 to other uses of the verb throughout the Apostolic Writings, sometimes also consulting the Septuagint. This provides a larger body of witness than Matthew's Gospel alone while still retaining the useful constraint of only consulting canonical writings, which limits the uses studied to those which are still relatively useful and contemporary. However, a full consultation of all appearances of the word within the Apostolic Writings and the Septuagint is a significant undertaking and includes numerous references which may be of dubious relevance to the study of Matthew 5:17, as revealed in the Biblical Overview. As such, few scholars argue that this is the best framework for interpreting Matthew 5:17, though

83 This conclusion is the result of the author's own survey of Early Christian texts, summarized in the section on πληρόω as used in ancient Greek literature.

84 Trout, "Nature," 4.

85 Trout, "Community," 3.

this framework is informative by way of reminder that sources contemporary to and addressing a similar subject as the disputed use of πληρόω (*pleroo*) are helpful for clarification, even if those other sources are from a different author.

Based on the strengths and weaknesses of these frameworks, the theory adopted by the author attempts to create a method that will feature the same strengths as other methods of determining a relevant context for interpretation purposes while minimizing associated weaknesses. The framework which comes closest to realizing these goals is one which views the sayings of Jesus that contain πληρόω (*pleroo*) in all four Gospels as the most relevant context for interpreting the word as it is used in Matthew 5:17. This allows sayings from all four Gospels to be taken into account, limiting the context to four contemporary sources that all address similar subjects—the advantage of the approach of consulting the Apostolic Writings. The proposed framework also incorporates the advantage of the Matthew-based framework by following the work of one character in all four Gospel narratives, thereby consulting only the context from the Author of the statement in question, namely Jesus. This framework also avoids the key disadvantages of both the Matthew-based and Apostolic Writings frameworks. Unlike the Matthew-based framework, it avoids most of the fulfillment citations that have already been shown to be of less relevant context for Matthew 5:17. And unlike the broader Apostolic Writings framework, the context is limited to a small but still sufficient and relevant set of uses of πληρόω (*pleroo*).

Chapter 2

Research Approaches

Having outlined the limitations of the research and defined the topic in the Introduction, and having reviewed the relevant literature in Chapter 1, it is now necessary to outline the means of data collection and analysis that will be used to answer the main question of this book. This is the last matter of procedure before our in-depth survey of appearances of πληρόω (*pleroo*) in the sayings of Jesus can proceed. As a word study limited in scope to the analysis of twenty specific Biblical passages, the focus of the research will always remain on the text of Scripture. However, the research method outlined in this chapter will describe the appropriate process used for the collection and employment of secondary sources to provide a range of contrasting scholarly opinions and interpretations that may be used to clarify the best interpretation for the use of πληρόω (*pleroo*) in each verse examined.

Because the present study is dependent, at least in part, on the work of previous scholars, a large part of the analysis will involve assessing the quality of various sources. This will have the most significant impact of any part of the research on its conclusion, since these other scholars' opinions will serve as checks and balances to weigh against one another, as well as against the author's own position. As such, the delineation of research methods is critical to ensure the coherence, logical flow, and relevance of the research conducted in this work and its conclusion. Because of this, the delineation of research methods forms a vital part of the foundation on which the conclusion of the research will rest and must be explained both systematically and carefully.

This analysis of πληρόω (*pleroo*) as used in Matthew 5:17 focuses on the collection and compilation of existing data. The data collected will, in turn, be used to answer the main question of this book by the process of mutual comparison and contrast between the various views consulted, assessing which explanations best fit the context under scrutiny. Thus, the conclusion will be reached by means of inductive reasoning, presenting an argument with strong support to prove that the conclusion is very likely true.[1]

Research Process

In this descriptive study, one of the most significant potential threats to the strength of the conclusion is the quality of the sources from which data is derived. A study with good inductive reasoning from facts documented in sources of high quality yields a very strong argument, but if the study is too dependent on sources of low quality, the conclusion will have only weak support at best, and at worst be fallaciously arbitrary.[2] The best remedy against such a mistake is to comparatively analyze multiple sources to assess the relative quality, usefulness, and strength of argument in each.[3]

The ultimate aim of the comparative analysis in this word study is to examine multiple uses of πληρόω (*pleroo*) to clarify its meaning as it is used in one specific verse, namely Matthew 5:17. While the ultimate end of the research will be to define whether πληρόω (*pleroo*) should be understood to carry a constructive or destructive sense in Matthew 5:17, the research will still need to cover a broad range of uses and contexts for πληρόω (*pleroo*) because Jesus uses the word with multiple meanings and in different contexts, a fact which will be shown in Chapter 3. While the limitations previously established have reduced the scope to a useful and manageable area of study, it is still necessary to examine the nineteen

---

1 Nancy Jean Vyhmeister and Terry Dwain Robertson, *Your Guide to Writing Quality Research Papers: For Students of Religion and Theology* (Grand Rapids, MI: Zondervan, 2014), 105.

2 Jason Lisle, *The Ultimate Proof of Creation* (Green Forest, AR: Master, 2009), 134.

3 Vyhmeister and Robertson, *Research Papers*, 105.

other uses of πληρόω (*pleroo*) forms by Jesus and categorize them as more or less relevant to the use in Matthew 5:17.

As such, the analysis of these verses of Scripture will be of a very specific nature, examining the uses of πληρόω (*pleroo*) by Jesus in the Gospels for three primary data points. These data points will be unique to each passage and will be the result of the assessment and comparison of multiple scholarly sources with the passage and its context. Once the data points have been ascertained for each passage, the passages will be compared to determine which one contains the use of πληρόω (*pleroo*) that is closest in form and context to the use in Matthew 5:17. Then, the closest passage in meaning to Matthew 5:17 will be compared with that verse, answering the research question by using the similar passage to illuminate the meaning of πληρόω (*pleroo*) used in Matthew 5:17.

Data Points

Each passage will be assessed to determine what insight the context provides regarding whether the use of the πληρόω (*pleroo*) form is constructive, hybrid, or destructive. For this determination, the primary evidence considered will be the recipient of the verbal action of the πληρόω (*pleroo*) form, comparable uses from other literature, and the opinions of scholars and commentators on the meaning of each πληρόω (*pleroo*) form in its context. In this respect, evidence from commentators and other ancient literature will be considered secondary to evidence from the immediate context, but in the case of commentators and scholars, multiple relevant sources will be consulted to observe the degree of dispute or consensus on the use of πληρόω (*pleroo*) as constructive, hybrid, or destructive in each passage.

Each passage will also be analyzed for possible insights as to the specific definition of πληρόω (*pleroo*) as used in that passage. To this end, the clues gleaned from the research on the first data point will be compiled with further evidence from commentators and lexica to construct the most precise understanding possible regarding the meaning intended for πληρόω (*pleroo*) in the context of each passage. The goal of the research will be, at a minimum, to provide a precise definition in cases where the meaning of πληρόω (*pleroo*) in its context is abundantly clear and subject to minimal academic dispute.

Finally, these results will be assessed in conjunction with the context of the passage to see how favorably it might be viewed as a similar context and use as is found in Matthew 5:17. For this purpose, the best evidence will come from the immediate context of the πληρόω (*pleroo*) form in question and the specific inflected form of πληρόω (*pleroo*) used. The result will be an assessment of the passage in terms of its near or distant relevance for Matthew 5:17.[4] Based on the evidence gleaned from the research conducted in Chapter 1, passages with an abstract object for πληρόω (*pleroo*) and those which use the most similar inflected forms will be considered the passages of nearest relevance, while those with concrete objects for πληρόω (*pleroo*), citation formulae, and dissimilar inflected forms will be of most distant relevance.

In the analysis for collecting all three data points for each passage, the research will be guided by the works of other scholars who have considered each passage, the Biblical context in which each passage is found, and other related issues to analyze the scholars' opinions on these areas. This will permit an assessment of the uses of πληρόω (*pleroo*) that are relatively clear in meaning and undisputed in use by the scholarly community. In turn, this will permit the establishment of a base set of undisputed passages from which passages with more disputed uses ofπληρόω (*pleroo*) may be clarified, operating on the hermeneutical principle[5] of using the

4 J. Scott Duvall and J. Daniel Hays, *Grasping God's Word: A Hands-on Approach to Reading, Interpreting, and Applying the Bible* (Grand Rapids, MI: Zondervan Academic, 2020), 181.

5 *Hermeneutics* is the study and science of interpreting written documents. This book is interpreting the Bible with a historical-grammatical hermeneutic, which is a fancy way of saying that this book takes the Bible: (1) As the original author

clear to help define the unclear.[6] The comparison will also permit the assessment of various scholars' views with respect to each other to see who articulates the strongest and best-supported argument with respect to each data point.

Data Collection

Data for the research comes from an assortment of sources to permit consultation of multiple scholarly viewpoints on many of the issues assessed, with special emphasis on ensuring the appropriate representation of views from both sides of the debate regarding the use of πληρόω (*pleroo*) as constructive or destructive. This permits the gathering of a broad sample from scholarly perspectives, especially with respect to three centrally relevant topics for the research. First, sources providing insight on the general meaning of πληρόω (*pleroo*) are helpful for general categorization and grasping the semantic range of the word, as it encompasses constructive, hybrid, and destructive uses. Second, sources on the use of πληρόω (*pleroo*) in Matthew 5:17 provide a general overview of previous scholarly perspectives and often reveal underlying assumptions about which passages and contexts are most relevant for the interpretation of πληρόω (*pleroo*) in the verse that is the focus of study. Third and finally, sources that cover the uses of πληρόω (*pleroo*) in other passages from the Gospels where Jesus is the speaker form a key component of the main analysis in their assessments of other relevant uses of πληρόω (*pleroo*), providing perspective on the meaning of the verb independent from the polemical import of Matthew 5:17.

---

intended, (2) in the Bible's historical context, as the original audience would have understood, and (3) in the Bible's grammatical context, assuming the authors used the standard language and communication patterns of their day to get their message across clearly to their original audience.

6 Walter C. Kaiser Jr. and Moises Silva, *Introduction to Biblical Hermeneutics* (Grand Rapids, MI: Zondervan Academic, 2007), 247.

Data Analysis

The most important step for articulating a conclusion from the raw information consulted by this book is the subsequent analysis. This analysis will be performed based on sound hermeneutical practices, conducted in a manner that minimizes the expression of direct or indirect bias on the part of the author. While the selection of sources from multiple scholarly perspectives plays a major role in the reduction of bias, creating a set system for organizing the analysis and a formula for synthesizing the results of each area of research is another important factor, for this will ensure consistent representation and help with the fair characterization of each source consulted for the purposes of study.[7]

Organization of Research

With respect to organization and order of the analysis, the sources consulted for each area of the research will be grouped and analyzed based on the specific Biblical text or texts addressed by each source. This will provide the fairest comparison of data because the similarities and differences between various texts and scholarly interpretations of the same will be easiest to observe when comparing sources that speak of the same text and the same subject matter. This will also permit a general ordering of the research that passes through each Gospel from beginning to end, apart from Matthew 5:17. In order to place the analysis of Matthew 5:17 at the end while still analyzing the verse immediately after its nearest contexts in the Gospel of Matthew, the Gospels will be analyzed in the reverse of their canonical order, beginning with John and ending with Matthew.

For each passage, all the sources that address a given Biblical passage will be compared with one another to discover the range of scholarly opinions on the meaning of the πληρόω (*pleroo*) form in the passage.

---

7 William Badke, *Research Strategies: Finding Your Way Through the Information Fog* (Bloomington, IN: iUniverse, 2017), 306-30 7.

This will create an overview of scholarly opinions for each individual verse, noting which groups of scholars generally agree with one another and the ways in which scholars or groups may disagree. Such an assessment will provide preliminary options for the three data points, which are the objective of the analysis.

Once this survey of opinions is complete, each distinct perspective discernible among the scholarly opinions will be compared against the features of the Biblical text under scrutiny. This will permit the consideration of the features of grammar, syntax, and discourse present in each verse, offering possible clues and pieces of evidence that may contradict or have been overlooked by some or all of the scholarly perspectives surveyed. The analysis will show which scholarly opinions are most likely in view of the Biblical context and eliminate any spurious or unlikely options from the opinions surveyed, refining the preliminary options to those with the best potential for being the correct interpretation of the passage in question.

This will lead to the process of synthesizing the data and discovering which sources best explain the features of the Biblical text that may illuminate the use of the πληρόω (*pleroo*) form as constructive, hybrid, or destructive, the specific meaning of the πληρόω (*pleroo*) form under scrutiny with an appropriate gloss for translation, and the degree of similarity that the text under scrutiny has to the use of πληρόω (*pleroo*) in Matthew 5:17. In some of these data points, none of the scholarly opinions presented will provide a satisfactory explanation for the meaning of the πληρόω (*pleroo*) form, but this circumstance, while present, is rare. When a combination of multiple views or an entirely novel view provides a sufficiently superior explanation of the text over the singular view of a scholar or group, such a view will be noted and defended on textual grounds by means of the survey of the grammar, syntax, and discourse features that demand the different interpretation.

The assessment of the similarities and differences between sources as they relate to each passage will, in turn, reveal by process of logical evaluation which sources are of the best quality, the most relevant, and deliver the best argument.[8] In this process, a significant part of the logical evaluation will consist of an examination seeking to determine how well a given view matches any indicators embedded into the Biblical context for what that passage's use of πληρόω (*pleroo*) might mean. The sources that can be shown by comparison with both the Biblical context and the other sources to be the strongest will form the foundation of my conclusions.

Synthesis of Data

The result of this research process will be a detailed commentary on each of the twenty verses in the Gospels where Jesus uses forms of πληρόω (*pleroo*). The commentary will be specifically oriented toward discovering the correct interpretation of all three of the previously outlined data points, focusing on the ways in which each verse might be helpful for illuminating the meaning of πληρόω (*pleroo*) as it appears in Matthew 5:17. While other matters of interpretation will be considered wherever it is relevant for the discovery of the meaning of the πληρόω (*pleroo*) form in a given text, it is the meaning of the πληρόω (*pleroo*) form and its relevance for the interpretation of Matthew 5:17 that will always remain the central focus for each verse's commentary.

Because of the specific and centralized focus of the commentary, the analysis will present a synthesis of the research for each passage analyzed and provide a conclusion on whether the πληρόω (*pleroo*) form is used in a constructive, hybrid, or destructive manner, the most likely specific definition intended for the πληρόω (*pleroo*) form, and the degree of relevance of the given πληρόω (*pleroo*) form in its context as a parallel to Matthew 5:17. Once each relevant passage has been analyzed individually in Chapter 3, this evidence will be assessed as a whole in light of

8 Badke, *Research Strategies*, 261.

the scholarly opinions and the context of Matthew 5:17 in Chapter 4. Based on the weight of evidence as uncovered in the contexts of Jesus' utterances in which πληρόω (*pleroo*) appears that are most similar to His use of the term in Matthew 5:17, the research will arrive at its final conclusion as to whether πληρόω (*pleroo*) is used in a constructive, hybrid, or destructive manner in Matthew 5:17, observing whether or not it is possible to comment on the precise meaning and possible translative glosses for the word in that context.

Chapter 3

The Sayings of Yeshua

With the subject of research defined, the topic narrowed, more general studies of meaning complete, and a fixed procedure of research defined, now it is possible to address the central focus of our study, namely the meanings of πληρόω (*pleroo*) as the verb is used by Jesus throughout the Gospels. In this chapter, nineteen of the twenty uses of πληρόω (*pleroo*) by Jesus will be examined, with Matthew 5:17 excluded to be covered on its own in Chapter 4. In this way, the data points gleaned from all nineteen other uses can be utilized to clarify the main disputed passage under scrutiny, giving the greatest likelihood for providing a final resolution to the research question. Each analysis begins with the verse presented in Greek and English, with the πληρόω (*pleroo*) form and its English translation written in **bold** to make it easier to find. The English translation is my own, so you may wish to look up each verse in your favorite Bible as well.

The Gospel of John

The use of πληρόω (*pleroo*) forms is attributed to Jesus most frequently in the Gospel of John, where He uses forms of the verb eight times in seven passages. Notably, Jesus most frequently employs middle or passive forms of πληρόω (*pleroo*) in this Gospel, with only the occurrence in John 16:6 containing an active form of πληρόω (*pleroo*). Thus, while most of the forms in John have a limitation of relevance for Matthew 5:17 due to the differences in inflection, some of the πληρόω (*pleroo*) forms used by Jesus in this Gospel are still helpful due to their proximity with other key words also found in the context of Matthew 5:17.

1. My Time is Not Yet Complete: John 7:8

> ὑμεῖς ἀνάβητε εἰς τὴν ἑορτήν· ἐγὼ ⸀οὐκ ἀναβαίνω εἰς τὴν ἑορτὴν ταύτην, ὅτι ὁ ἐμὸς καιρὸς ⸀οὔπω **πεπλήρωται.** (NA28)
>
> You all go up to the feast, I will not yet go up to this feast, since My time is not yet **complete**. (Author's Translation)

In this passage, Jesus objects to the suggestion by His brothers that He go up publicly to Jerusalem for the Feast of Tabernacles with the words "My time is not yet complete" (Author's translation). Here, the object of the πληρόω (*pleroo*) form is καιρὸς (*kairos*), which means "time."[1] This idea of time is the central focus of Jesus' discourse, and the use of πεπλήρωται (pronounced *pe-play-ro-tie*, transliterated *peplerotai*) in this verse is a parallel intensification of His use of πάρεστιν (pronounced *par-es-tin*, transliterated *parestin*) in John 7:6.[2] πάρειμι (pronounced *pa-ray-me*, transliterated *pareimi*), defined "to be present" or "to be available," speaks of the impersonal καιρὸς (*kairos*) and carries the metaphorical connotation of "come, arrive."[3] Since πεπλήρωται (*peplerotai*) is used to refer to the same event, the word carries a destructive meaning and may be glossed as "complete."

In this respect, all commentators consulted agree that this use of πληρόω (*pleroo*) is destructive, including Bernard,[4] Harris,[5] Thompson,[6]

---

1 BDAG, s.v., "καιρὸς," 1:497.
2 Edward W. Klink, *John*, ECNT (Grand Rapids, MI: Zondervan, 2016), 354.
3 BDAG, s.v., "πάρειμι," 1:773.
4 Bernard, *St. John*, 270.
5 Murray J. Harris, *John*, EGGNT (Nashville, TN: B&H Academic, 2015), 151–152.
6 Marianne Meye Thompson, *John: A Commentary*, NTL (Louisville, KY: Westminster John Knox, 2015), 168.

Talbert,[7] and Klink.[8] While the object of this πληρόω (*pleroo*) form is abstract, the form used is a third-person singular perfect passive indicative, which differs in tense, voice, and mood from the form used in Matthew 5:17. This does not render the verse completely irrelevant, but the dissimilar context and highly dissimilar inflected form do reduce the significance of this verse for the present study.

2. So That the Scripture May be Lived Out: John 13:18

> Οὐ περὶ πάντων ὑμῶν λέγω· ἐγὼ οἶδα ⸀τίνας ἐξελεξάμην· ἀλλ' ἵνα ἡ γραφὴ **πληρωθῇ**· ὁ τρώγων ⸁μου τὸν ἄρτον ⸀ἐπῆρεν °ἐπ' ἐμὲ τὴν πτέρναν αὐτοῦ. (NA28)
>
> I do not speak about all of you; I know who I chose; but this is so that the writing may **be lived out**, "The one eating bread with me lifted up his heel against me." (Author's Translation)

Here the πληρόω (*pleroo*) form is used in a citation formula for Psalm 41:9. The expected third-person singular aorist passive subjunctive is used, making this a standard quotation formula used by Jesus.[9] Although at first glance this could lead to the conclusion that this use is hybrid, it is important to observe the way this Scripture citation is used within the text of the Gospel. Although the text implies that Judas' actions would fulfill the Psalm quoted, the context of the Psalm is not predictive, a fact noted by Charry in her commentary on the Psalms.[10] Because of this fact, it is clear that the citation in this verse is an excellent example of a

---

7 Charles H. Talbert, *Reading John: A Literary and Theological Commentary on the Fourth Gospel and the Johannine Epistles* (Macon, Georgia: Smyth & Helwys, 2005), 150.

8 Klink, *John*, 355.

9 Harris, *John*, 247.

10 Ellen T. Charry, *Psalms 1-50*, BTC (Grand Rapids, MI: Brazos, 2015), 217.

typological citation of the OT, where the NT cites an OT passage that speaks of a trait of human nature and provides further commentary or a specific example of that trait.[11]

Because of the typological nature of this citation, nothing in Jesus' speech prevents the application of the same Scriptural passage to other people and events.[12] Rather, Jesus is citing Judas as one, and possibly the chief, example of several people who exemplify this Biblical type of a traitorous close friend. Other examples of this type include the sons of David, Absalom and Adonijah (2 Samuel 15, 1 Kings 1 NASB95). As such, this use is constructive and can be glossed as "to be accomplished," or perhaps more interpretively, "be done, be lived out." While the unique formulaic use and differing inflected form limit the direct relevance of this verse to Matthew 5:17, it serves as a useful reminder that even formulaic uses of a word are heavily affected by their contexts. What is more, this use is a good example of a possible definitional emphasis within the πληρόω (*pleroo*) lexeme, where the word is used to illustrate the most archetypical or consummate example of a type. More will be shown on this matter in the discussion of Matthew 3:15.

3. Your Joy May be Made Full: John 15:11

> Ταῦτα λελάληκα ὑμῖν ἵνα ἡ χαρὰ ἡ ἐμὴ ἐν ὑμῖν ⸀ᾖ καὶ ἡ χαρὰ ὑμῶν **πληρωθῇ**. (NA28)
>
> I spoke these things to you so that My joy may be in you, and your joy may be **made full**. (Author's translation)

Although this verse uses the same inflected form as John 13:18, the recipient of the verb's action is the abstract χαρὰ (*chara*, pronouncing the

11 Klink, *John*, 586.
12 Charry, *Psalms 1-50*, 217.

"ch" with a Scottish accent), which means "joy."[13] In the context, Jesus is referring to the completion, perfection, and filling up of joy for the apostles.[14] Since this emphasizes the process of filling and denotes an additive sense, this represents a constructive use for the term. Among the commentaries, Borchert,[15] Harris,[16] Thompson,[17] and Klink[18] agree that this form of πληρόω (*pleroo*) is used constructively here, while Talbert glosses over verse 11 and focuses his comments on other parts of the discourse.[19]

While the inflected form here is very different from that found in the Matthew passage, this use of πληρόω (*pleroo*) is not part of a citation formula. This fact makes it more relevant to the use in Matthew 5:17, because both verses feature a form of πληρόω (*pleroo*) in ordinary discourse. Because of this, both uses will carry a meaning for πληρόω (*pleroo*) that falls closer to the basic meaning of the word than a use of πληρόω (*pleroo*) in a formulaic citation, as shown in the preliminary study of other Greek literature.

4. So the Word in Their Law Might be Fulfilled: John 15:25

> ἀλλ' ἵνα **πληρωθῇ** ὁ λόγος ὁ ⸀ἐν τῷ νόμῳ αὐτῶν γεγραμμένος⸀ ὅτι ἐμίσησάν με δωρεάν. (NA28)

> But this they did so that the word written in their law might **be lived out** that, "they hated me freely." (Author's Translation)

---

13 BDAG, s.v., "χαρὰ," 1:1077.

14 Harris, *John*, 269.

15 Gerald L. Borchert, *John 12:21: An Exegetical and Theological Exposition of Holy Scripture*, NAC (Nashville, TN: B&H, 2002), 131.

16 Harris, *John*, 269.

17 Thompson, *John*, 327.

18 Klink, *John*, 656.

19 Talbert, *Reading John*, 222.

As with John 13:18, this use of πληρωθῇ (pronounced *play-ro-they,* transliterated *plerothe*) occurs in a citation from the Tanach, though it is debated whether the verse in view is Psalm 69:4 or Psalm 35:19.[20] However, the pericope consulted places strong limits on any potential destructive aspect for this πληρόω (*pleroo*) form. This is because, regardless of which Psalm is in view, the citation is typological in nature and not predictive.[21] Thus, while an instance of the phenomenon noted by the Psalmist came to pass in the world's rejection of Jesus, and this rejection is the greatest manifestation of the phenomenon, this citation is not precluding the application of the Psalms in question to other times where similar phenomena take place.[22]

Because of this fact, while the use of πληρόω (*pleroo*) here is hybrid, for all practical purposes it is constructive due to the minimal emphasis placed on the destructive aspect of the word's meaning. This is noted in Klink[23] and Thompson[24] but glossed over in Harris[25] and Borchert.[26] Talbert disagrees, arguing that a destructive aspect should be read into the verb with a suggested interpretive gloss of "accomplish."[27] However, Talbert appears to view this citation as predictive, failing to note the possibility that it might be typological. Due to this oversight, Klink's view that the πληρόω (*pleroo*) form is constructive is superior.

The translative gloss is the same as John 13:18, but one factor that makes this passage slightly more relevant for Matthew 5:17 is that despite the difference in verbal forms and formulaic use of πληρόω (*pleroo*), this

---

20 Harris, *John*, 273.

21 As seen in Thompson, *John*, 333–334. Thompson argues that both Psalms 35 and 69 are in view and that both Psalms taken together provide a fuller picture for the typological citation.

22 Klink, *John*, 667.

23 Klink, *John*, 667.

24 Thompson, *John*, 334.

25 Harris, *John*, 273.

26 Borchert, *John*, 139–140.

27 Talbert, *Reading John*, 224.

verse uses the verb under study in proximity to an interesting use of νόμος (*nomos*), which means "law."[28]

The full citation formula used in this verse is "ἀλλ' ἵνα πληρωθῇ ὁ λόγος ὁ ἐν τῷ νόμῳ αὐτῶν γεγραμμένος ὅτι…" (NA28), (transliterated, "*All' hina plerothe ho logos ho en to nomo auton gegrammenos hoti…*") "But [this they did] so the word written in their law might be fulfilled…" (Author's translation). The fact that this citation comes from the Psalms and not from the Torah proves that this use of νόμος (*nomos*) carries a general sense, referring to the entire canonical unit of the Hebrew Scriptures.[29] This broader use for νόμος (*nomos*) is important to keep in mind, for although the noun occurs as part of a different formulaic expression in Matthew 5:17, the meaning of νόμος (*nomos*) there is the same as in this verse, a fact which will be demonstrated in Chapter 4.

5. Sorrow Filled Your Hearts: John 16:6

> ἀλλ' ὅτι ταῦτα λελάληκα ὑμῖν ἡ λύπη **πεπλήρωκεν** ὑμῶν τὴν καρδίαν. (NA28)
>
> But because I said this to you, sorrow **filled** your hearts. (Author's Translation)

The use of πληρόω (*pleroo*) in this verse represents the only time in John's Gospel where Yeshua uses an active form of the verb under scrutiny, a third-person singular perfect active indicative. While this is not an identical inflected form to Matthew 5:17, the fact that both forms are in the active voice increases the relevance of this verse for understanding Matthew 5:17. Although in most uses it is the Object of this verb that helps determine its use, in this case both the Object καρδίαν (*kardian*),

---

28 BDAG, s.v., "νόμος," 1:677.
29 Borchert, *John*, 140.

"hearts,"[30] as well as the Subject λύπη (pronounced *loo-pay*, transliterated *lupe*), "sorrow," which reveal the meaning of the πληρόω (*pleroo*) form in this verse.[31] The use is abstract and refers to the filling of a person with emotion, with wide attestation in the Septuagint and other ancient literature.[32]

While Borchert[33] and Talbert[34] gloss over the πληρόω (*pleroo*) form, Harris,[35] Thompson,[36] and Klink[37] agree that the specific use in this case speaks of control, that grief has filled the hearts of the disciples to the point of controlling them and their thoughts. Given the active form of this verb, however, the emphasis would be on the process of grief gaining control over the disciples, and as the next verse reveals, Jesus is attempting to make them aware of this process so they can resume control over the feelings of grief.[38] This marks a constructive use of πληρόω (*pleroo*), in a verse that is relevant to Matthew 5:17 due to its abstract referent and matching voice.

6. Your Joy May be Made Complete: John 16:24

> ἕως ἄρτι οὐκ ᾐτήσατε οὐδὲν ἐν τῷ ὀνόματί μου· ⸀αἰτεῖτε καὶ λήμψεσθε, ἵνα ἡ χαρὰ ὑμῶν ᾖ **πεπληρωμένη**. (NA28)
>
> Until now you have asked for nothing in My name; ask and you will receive, so that your joy **becomes complete**. (Author's Translation)

---

30 BDAG, s.v., "καρδία," 1:508.
31 BDAG, s.v., "λύπη," 1:605.
32 BDAG, s.v., "πληρόω" 1:828.
33 Borchert, *John*, 145.
34 Talbert, *Reading John*, 226.
35 Harris, *John*, 276.
36 Thompson, *John*, 337.
37 Klink, *John*, 677.
38 Klink, *John*, 677.

This use is like the one in John 15:11 in that the recipient of the verbal action, χαρὰ (*chara*) is the same in both cases and that both forms of the verb are in the passive singular. However, the inflected form is different in that this verse uses a participle instead of the subjunctive verb used in John 15:11. Among the commentaries, there is disagreement as to whether this difference in inflected form shifts the emphasis of the verb from the process to its result. Borchert[39] and Harris[40] maintain that the participle places emphasis on the result of the process, leading to a hybrid interpretation of the πληρόω (*pleroo*) form that emphasizes the destructive aspect of the verb.

While Klink does not directly address the issue of the participle, his comments are more process-focused, suggesting that he understands the participle to carry an import similar to the subjunctive in John 15:11, thereby supporting a constructive interpretation of the πληρόω (*pleroo*) form.[41] Both Talbert[42] and Thompson[43] gloss over the verb and do not address the matter. In this case, the view of Borchert and Harris has stronger textual grounds. As such, it is preferable to take the πληρόω (*pleroo*) form as hybrid, with a slightly greater emphasis on the destructive aspect of the verb's semantic range.[44] Like John 15:11, however, the use of the passive voice limits the relevance of this use for Matthew 5:17, though without rendering this verse entirely irrelevant.

7. Scripture Fulfilled and Filled with His Joy: John 17:12–13

ὅτε ἤμην μετ᾽ αὐτῶν ⊤ ἐγὼ ἐτήρουν αὐτοὺς ἐν τῷ ὀνόματί
⸀σου ⸂ᾧ δέδωκάς μοι, καὶ⸃ ἐφύλαξα, καὶ οὐδεὶς °ἐξ αὐτῶν

39 Borchert, *John*, 155.

40 Harris, *John*, 281–282.

41 Klink, *John*, 692.

42 Talbert, *Reading John*, 229.

43 Thompson, *John*, 344.

44 Borchert, *John*, 155; Harris, *John*, 281–282.

> ἀπώλετο εἰ μὴ ὁ υἱὸς τῆς ἀπωλείας, ἵνα ἡ γραφὴ **πληρωθῇ**. νῦν δὲ πρὸς σὲ ἔρχομαι καὶ ταῦτα λαλῶ ἐν τῷ κόσμῳ ἵνα ἔχωσιν τὴν χαρὰν τὴν ἐμὴν **πεπληρωμένην** ⸀ἐν ἑαυτοῖς⸁. (NA28)
>
> While I was with them, I guarded those you gave Me in Your Name, and I guarded them, and not one of them was lost except the son of destruction, so that the writing **might come to pass**. But now I come to You and I say this in the word, so that they may have My joy **filling** them **up**. (Author's Translation)

This passage represents the only occasion in the Gospels where Yeshua uses πληρόω (*pleroo*) in two consecutive verses. Although these two uses are very close to one another in proximity, it is interesting to note that the meanings for each of these two forms are very different. While both forms are separated from the inflection of the πληρόω (*pleroo*) form in Matthew 5:17 by a greater degree than that shown for other uses of πληρόω (*pleroo*) by Yeshua in John's Gospel, these two forms in proximity present a compelling demonstration of both the semantic range of πληρόω (*pleroo*) and the heavy dependence on context displayed in the meaning of this verb.

i. So That the Writing Might be Fulfilled: John 17:12. Because the recipient of the verbal action of the πληρόω (*pleroo*) form in this sentence is ἡ γραφὴ (pronounced *hey gra-fey*, transliterated *he graphe*), "the writing," it would at first appear to be the same formulaic use seen in John 13:18 and 15:25, marking a citation of Scripture.[45] However, unlike these other two passages in this verse there is no quotation and not even a hint as to what Scripture may be in mind within the text.[46] However, the encasement of πληρωθῇ (*plerothe*) within the formulaic phrase is strong enough evidence for many to conclude that the citation formula

---

45 BDAG, s.v., "γραφὴ," 1:206.

46 Borchert, *John*, 173.

itself constitutes an allusion to the Tanach,[47] and Thompson suggests that the passage in view is the same as that cited in John 13:18, thereby explaining the abbreviated nature of this citation.[48] While it is clear this use is some kind of hybrid and that the word is best glossed "come to pass," the weight of the sentence does not rest on any sort of emphasis towards a more constructive or destructive meaning, leading to the conclusion that attempting to discern such an import would be more eisegesis than exegesis in this case.

ii. So That They May be Filled with My Joy: John 17:13. Like John 15:11 and 16:24, the recipient of the verbal action of this πληρόω (*pleroo*) form is χαρὰ (*chara*). The inflected form here is also nearly identical to the one in John 16:24, differing only in that this participle is in the accusative case while the one in John 16:24 is in the nominative. As such, verse 16:24 is an excellent controlling context from which to interpret John 17:13, a matter which is confirmed by the observation that other scholars' comments on the use of πληρόω (*pleroo*) in John 16:24 match closely with their comments on the πληρόω (*pleroo*) form in John 17:13.[49] Based on this, it is sound to reason that the present use of πληρόω (*pleroo*) is hybrid, with an emphasis on the destructive aspect of the verb's semantic range as shown in Hera's exposition.[50] Such an interpretation places the focus of Jesus' words on the resultant state of the disciples' being filled with joy.[51] The best gloss is "filled," with the abstract object indicating the conceptual use of this term, and like John 16:24, it is of limited relevance to Matthew 5:17.

---

47 This is true although there is significant dispute as to which passage may be in view. See Borchert, *John*, 173; Harris, *John*, 289; Klink, *John*, 719.

48 Thompson, *John*, 354.

49 The best example of this is Klink, *John*, 692, 720.

50 Marianus Pale Hera, "Christology and Discipleship in John 17" (PhD diss., Catholic University of America, 2012), 217, ProQuest (AAT 3544251).

51 Klink, *John*, 720.

The Gospel of Luke

In the Gospel of Luke, Jesus uses forms of πληρόω (*pleroo*) a total of four times. All four occurrences are passive. In the case of Luke 24:44, this difference in voice is the only difference in inflection with the form in Matthew 5:17. Moreover, this verse features a recipient of the verbal action that is very similar to the recipient of the same verb's action in Matthew 5:17. As such, there is still much information which can be learned from the uses of πληρόω (*pleroo*) by Yeshua in Luke that for the most part supports the traditional interpretations of Matthew 5:17.

1. This Scripture is Accomplished in Your Hearing: Luke 4:21

> ἤρξατο δὲ λέγειν πρὸς αὐτοὺς °ὅτι σήμερον **πεπλήρωται** ἡ γραφὴ αὕτη ἐν τοῖς ὠσὶν ὑμῶν. (NA28)
>
> But He began to say to them that "today this writing **is accomplished** in all your hearing." (Author's Translation)

In this verse ἡ γραφὴ (*he graphe*) is the recipient of the verbal action in the πληρόω (*pleroo*) form, but a feature which makes this passage stand out is that this reference to Scripture is not a citation formula but is instead a declarative statement by Jesus.[52] As such, this passage is distinct from most of those which use πληρόω (*pleroo*) in a citation formula, where the citation forms a narratorial aside. Based on the word of Frein, Garland suggests that Jesus is referring to His miracles and ministry highlighted later in Luke's Gospel as the fulfillment of the passage Jesus read in verse 18.[53]

---

52 Walter L. Liefeld and David W. Pao, *Luke*, EBC (Grand Rapids, MI: Zondervan, 2007), 4:21.

53 David E. Garland, *Luke*, ECNT (Grand Rapids, MI: Zondervan, 2011), 200.

However, most other scholars, including Thompson,[54] Liefeld and Pao,[55] and Perrin[56] argue that Jesus cannot be referring to later events because such a view is not supported by the grammar of the passage. These scholars argue that the passage places its grammatical emphasis on the present implications of the verbal action, and that because of this, it is far more likely based on the context of verse 4:23 that Jesus was referring to His past and current signs and miracles as the fulfillment of Isaiah 61, and that the present effect implied by the perfect tense of πεπλήρωται (*peplerotai*) is His reputation as a miracle-worker.

Based on the use of the perfect-tense πεπλήρωται (*peplerotai*) in this verse in combination with the preceding adverb σήμερον (*semeron*), the grammar does offer strongest support to the majority scholarly view that Jesus refers to His past and present acts with the πληρόω (*pleroo*) form of this verse. As such, Luke 4:21 contains a hybrid use of πληρόω (*pleroo*) that is best glossed "fulfill," "accomplish," or "perform." While the reference to Scripture bears a partial similarity to Matthew 5:17, the difference in inflected form of πληρόω (*pleroo*) means it is possible that the verbs communicate different meanings in each verse.

2. The Completion of the Times of the Gentiles: Luke 21:241

> καὶ πεσοῦνται στόματι ⸀μαχαίρης καὶ αἰχμαλωτισθήσονται εἰς τὰ ἔθνη πάντα, καὶ Ἰερουσαλὴμ ἔσται πατουμένη ὑπὸ ἐθνῶν, ἄχρι οὗ **πληρωθῶσιν** ⸆ ⸋καιροὶ ἐθνῶν⸌. (NA28)
>
> And they will fall by the mouth of the sword, and they will be put into captivity into all the nations, and Jerusalem will be

54 Alan J. Thompson, *Luke*, EGGNT (Nashville, TN: B&H Academic, 2016), 74–75.

55 Liefeld and Pao, *Luke*, 4:21.

56 Nicholas Perrin, *Luke: An Introduction and Commentary*, TNTC (Downers Grove, IL: InterVarsity, 2022), 4:20–21.

> trampled under the nations, until the times of the nations **are completed**. (Author's Translation)

The recipient of the verbal action of this verse's πληρόω (*pleroo*) form is καιροὶ ἐθνῶν (*kairoi ethnon*), "the times of the Gentiles" (Luke 21:24 NASB95). As such, this represents a destructive use of the verb that refers to the closure of the specified time. Although scholars debate the meaning of the reference to "the times of the Gentiles," Thompson,[57] Garland,[58] Liefeld and Pao,[59] Perrin,[60] Smith,[61] and Johnson[62] all agree that this πληρόω (*pleroo*) form is both temporal and destructive.

Although this verb is the same tense as the πληρόω (*pleroo*) form in Matthew 5:17, all other aspects of inflection are different. Further, the recipient of the verbal action in this case is indicative of a specialized, possibly formulaic use of πληρόω (*pleroo*), for as shown in the preceding chapter the use of πληρόω (*pleroo*) with any kind of time as the recipient of the verbal action carries the sense of ending the time period specified. Because of these things, this use has relatively little relevance for understanding the use of πληρόω (*pleroo*) in Matthew 5:17.

3. Until it is Performed in the Kingdom: Luke 22:16

> λέγω γὰρ ὑμῖν °ὅτι ⸀οὐ μὴ φάγω⸃ ⸀αὐτὸ ἕως ὅτου ⸀**πληρωθῇ** ἐν τῇ βασιλείᾳ τοῦ θεοῦ. (NA28)

57 Thompson, *Luke*, 134.

58 Garland, *Luke*, 868.

59 Liefeld and Pao, *Luke*, 21:20–24.

60 Perrin, *Luke*, 21:24b.

61 Steve Smith, *The Fate of the Jerusalem Temple in Luke-Acts: An Intertextual Approach to Jesus' Laments Over Jerusalem and Stephen's Speech* (London: Bloomsbury T&T Clark, 2017), 90.

62 Luke Timothy Johnson, *Sacra Pagina: The Gospel of Luke* (Collegeville, MN: Liturgical, 1991), 324.

> For I say to you all that I will never ever eat it until **it is performed** in the kingdom of God." (Author's Translation)

This use of πληρόω (*pleroo*) represents one of the most difficult in the NT. Often, commentators choose to simply gloss πληρωθῇ (*plerothe*) as "it is fulfilled" without providing further explanation of the meaning of this use of the verb.[63] Those that do comment on the matter argue that the verb's sense is temporal and eschatological, including Thompson,[64] Perrin,[65] and Bock.[66] If this sense is taken, the general verbal meaning would be destructive, in a context that has some relevance for Matthew 5:17.

However, there is one major challenge to this conventional view. The most commonly adopted reading of this passage understands the πληρόω (*pleroo*) form to carry a meaning of "bring to an end, complete," but elsewhere this meaning is exclusively attested in cases where the recipient of the verbal action is some kind of time. While the idea of time is present in Luke 22:16, the recipient of the verbal action of πληρωθῇ (*plerothe*) is the antecedent of the pronoun αὐτὸ (pronounced *ow-to*, transliterated *auto*). There is some debate about the antecedent, for Liefeld and Pao argue that the antecedent is the Passover Lamb while Thompson suggests that τὸ πάσχα (pronounced *ta pas-cha* with Scottish accent on the *ch*, transliterated as *pascha*), "the Passover," is the antecedent, implying the entire Passover meal.[67]

The broader context supports Thompson's view of the antecedent, as the Passover lamb is never specifically mentioned in Luke's account of the Passover, but other elements of the meal, notably the bread and wine, are (Luke 22:17–20.) Based on this understanding of the recipient of the

---

63 For example Garland, *Luke*, 890.

64 Thompson, *Luke*, 342.

65 Perrin, *Luke*, 22:16.

66 Darrell L. Bock, *Luke* (Grand Rapids, MI: Zondervan, 1996), 65.

67 Thompson, *Luke*, 342.

verbal action, the passage with the most similar recipient is Luke 4:21, which uses the verb in reference to Scripture with the gloss "accomplish, perform." This meaning squares well with the immediate context of Luke 22:16, as the parallel statement regarding the fruit of the vine in verse 18 implies that Yeshua will drink from the fruit of the vine at the coming of the kingdom of God, in the same way that He will eat, or "perform," the Passover at such time.[68] As such, the assertion by Thompson that this passage does not speak of a future keeping of the Passover sacrifice stands on textually weak grounds, as does the majority's destructive interpretation of πληρόω (*pleroo*).[69]

If the use of πληρόω (*pleroo*) in Luke 22:16 is understood with a similar meaning as the form used in Luke 4:21, this yields a gloss of "perform" and represents a constructive use of πληρόω (*pleroo*). Although the recipient of the verbal action is different, another analogous use to this one is John 13:18, a verse which uses the same inflected form as is found here. Although it is theoretically possible for Luke 22:16 to represent an occurrence of a type of temporal use of πληρόω (*pleroo*) that is not amply attested in other ancient Greek literature, the fact that an alternative meaning with relevant attestation in the Gospels is available makes such a proposition unlikely, and on these grounds, it is best to take this πληρόω (*pleroo*) form as constructive, with a gloss of "perform." While the passive inflected form affects the relevance of this verse for interpreting Matthew 5:17, the recipient of the verbal action is similar in concept. As such, this is one of the more relevant uses of πληρόω (*pleroo*) by Yeshua in Luke's Gospel for understanding Matthew 5:17, though as will be seen, there is one verse that is more relevant still.

---

68 Thompson, *Luke*, 342.

69 Thompson, *Luke*, 342.

4. It is Necessary to Perform All the Things Written: Luke 24:44

> Εἶπεν δὲ πρὸς αὐτούς· οὗτοι οἱ λόγοι μου οὓς ἐλάλησα πρὸς ὑμᾶς ⸀ἔτι ὢν⸀ σὺν ὑμῖν, ὅτι δεῖ **πληρωθῆναι** πάντα τὰ γεγραμμένα ἐν τῷ νόμῳ Μωϋσέως καὶ ⸀τοῖς προφήταις καὶ ψαλμοῖς περὶ ἐμοῦ. (NA28)

> But He said to them, 'These are My words which I spoke to you all while I was still with you, that it is necessary for all the things written in the Law of Moses and the Prophets and the Psalms about Me **to be accomplished**. (Author's Translation)

The most critical matter for interpreting this use of πληρόω (*pleroo*) is in the immediate context of the verse at hand, in Luke 24:46. Verse 46 enumerates specifically the prophecies Yeshua has in view when He makes the statement in verse 44 that He fulfilled all the things written about Him in Scripture.[70] The recipient of the verbal action of the πληρόω (*pleroo*) form is a full phrase here, τὰ γεγραμμένα ἐν τῷ νόμῳ Μωϋσέως καὶ ⸀τοῖς προφήταις καὶ ψαλμοῖς περὶ ἐμοῦ (Luke 24:44, NA28) (transliterated *ta gegrammena en to nomo Mouseos kai tois prophetais kai psalmois peri emou*), "the things written in the Law of Moses and the Prophets and Psalms about Me" (Luke 24:44, Author's translation). This phrase, and specifically the combined references to the Law, the Prophets, and the Psalms reveals that Christ is speaking of the entire Tanach as in John 15:25, though the use of the Psalms as a metonym for the Writings may be purposeful on Luke's part.[71]

Verse 46 goes further by defining the limiting clause from verse 44, περὶ ἐμοῦ (*peri emou*), by specifying the specific things prophesied in the Tanach concerning Messiah that Jesus has in view. Although Perrin argues

---

70 Thompson, *Luke*, 379.
71 Garland, *Luke*, 1008.

that the emphasis of the verb is on the climactic nature of Jesus' mission, denoting it as the climax of human history,[72] the contextual information from verse 46 makes it clear that at least the majority of the instances Jesus has in mind are predictive prophecies specific to His coming and work, a fact noted by Thompson[73] as well as Liefeld and Pao.[74] In this light, the use of πληρόω (*pleroo*) in this verse is most like the citation formula use, and the most relevant parallel passages are John 7:8, 15:25, and 17:12. On these grounds, the use of πληρόω (*pleroo*) in Luke 24:44 is destructive, with a gloss of "accomplish" or "perform." Although the verbal form is passive here, the recipient of the verbal action is substantially the same as that in Matthew 5:17, and in all matters of inflection besides voice, the verbal forms are the same between the two verses. As such, this verse is significant and relevant for the study of Matthew 5:17. Because it provides substantive support for the notion that the use of πληρόω (*pleroo*) in Matthew 5:17 is destructive, any attempt to argue otherwise must provide a reasonable answer for why this passage would differ in meaning from Matthew 5:17.

The Gospel of Mark

The Gospel in which Yeshua uses forms of πληρόω (*pleroo*) least frequently in His discourses is Mark, where the verb is used by Christ on only two occasions. Both uses are specialized and represent destructive uses that are well attested within the chapter two survey of the Septuagint and other Greek literature, namely the use of πληρόω (*pleroo*) to mark the close of a period of time and the use of πληρόω (*pleroo*) to indicate the occurrence of an event foretold by the prophets of the Lord. Because of the small number of occurrences and the exclusively specialized uses that appear in

72 Perrin, *Luke*, 24:44.

73 Thompson, *Luke*, 49, 379.

74 Liefeld and Pao, *Luke*, 24:44.

Mark, this Gospel is the least relevant for studying Jesus' use of πληρόω (*pleroo*) in relation to Matthew 5:17.

1. Saying The Time is Complete: Mark 1:15

> ⸀καὶ λέγων⸁ ὅτι ⸂**πεπλήρωται** ὁ καιρὸς⸃ καὶ ἤγγικεν ἡ βασιλεία τοῦ θεοῦ· μετανοεῖτε καὶ πιστεύετε ἐν τῷ εὐαγγελίῳ. (NA28)

> ...and saying that "the time **is complete** and the kingdom of God has come near; you all must repent and trust in the good news." (Author's Translation)

The recipient of the verbal action of this πληρόω (*pleroo*) form is ὁ καιρὸς (*ho kairos*), "the time."[75] Because of this, Mark 1:15 has much in common with Luke 21:24 and John 7:8, as all three share the same recipient of the verbal action. Although this suggests that the use of πληρόω (*pleroo*) here is destructive, there is debate among scholars on this point. Stein[76] notes that the focus is more on the arrival of the Kingdom of God than on the passing of the preceding age, which corroborates the view of Schnabel who argues the phrase means either the passing of a decisive moment or the end of a span of time.[77] In contrast, Jarvis and Johnson argue that the emphasis rests on the closure of a season in the history of God's redemptive work.[78]

---

75 BDAG, s.v., "καιρός," 1:497.

76 Robert H. Stein, *Mark Testament*, BECNT (Grand Rapids, MI: Baker Academic, 2008), 73.

77 Eckhard J. Schnabel, *Mark: An Introduction and Commentary*, TNTC (Downers Grove, IL: IVP Academic, 2015), 70.

78 Cynthia A. Jarvis and E. Elizabeth Johnson, *Feasting on the Gospels: Mark* (Louisville, KY: Westminster John Knox, 2014), 20.

Each perspective features its own unique challenges. Stein's view requires an interpretation of πληρόω (*pleroo*) that is inconsistent with its other uses in relation to καιρὸς (*kairos*), while Schnabel's leads to an imprecise understanding of what Jesus' proclamation in this verse could mean. Most seriously, Jarvis and Johnson's view adopts a view of καιρὸς (*kairos*) that requires a specialized rather than standard use. Fortunately, it is possible to combine the best of each opinion and argue that this use of πληρόω (*pleroo*) focuses on the closure of the preceding age, a view confirmed by Dillon.[79]

This view adopts the strength of Jarvis and Johnson's view in that it maintains a destructive interpretation of πληρόω (*pleroo*) that is consistent with the other uses of this verb in reference to time, in addition to the strength of Stein's view that does not require ὁ καιρὸς (*ho kairos*) to have any particular import, leaving the matter of whether the noun should be interpreted as "previous age" or "preceding salvation-historical season" to the broader context of Jesus' utterance. Further, the imprecision of Schnabel's view is avoided, providing the precise understanding of πληρόω (*pleroo*) as destructive with a gloss of "complete." The specialized use here in combination with an inflected form of πληρόω (*pleroo*) that is very different from that in Matthew 5:17 significantly reduces the relevance of Mark 1:15 for the Matthew passage.

2. This Happened so the Scriptures May be Fulfilled: Mark 14:49

> καθ' ἡμέραν ἤμην πρὸς ὑμᾶς ἐν τῷ ἱερῷ διδάσκων καὶ οὐκ ⸀ἐκρατήσατέ με· ἀλλ' ἵνα **πληρωθῶσιν** αἱ γραφαί. (NA28)

> I was with you people daily teaching in the Temple and you did not grab Me; but this happened so that the things written **may**

79 Richard J. Dillon, "Mark 1:1-15: A 'New Evangelization'?" *CBQ* 76, no. 1 (January 2014): 15.

come to pass. (Author's Translation)

This passage is very similar to John 15:25 and 17:12 in that there is debate over which Biblical passage may be in view within the citation formula. Moreover, like John 17:12, there is no section of the passage that represents a direct quote of the Tanach. However, the form of πληρόω (*pleroo*) used in this verse offers a clue in the fact that the third-person plural aorist passive subjunctive πληρωθῶσιν (pronounced *play-ro-tho-sin*, transliterated *plerothosin*) appears in place of the more common singular form πληρωθῇ (*plerothe*), and thus the close of Mark 14:49 may be translated "so that the Scriptures may be fulfilled." Due to the lack of obvious hints to a particular Tanach passage, scholars debate what reference might be intended.

Geddert[80] and Schnabel[81] suggest that Zechariah 13:17 is the most likely referent due to its having been cited previously by Jesus. Stein offers Isaiah 53:12 as an alternative to Zechariah 13:7 but favors the latter for the same reason as Geddert and Schnabel.[82] Jarvis and Johnson argue that the sentence is deliberately unfinished, and that the passage is purposefully ambiguous as to the Scripture being cited.[83] Interestingly, one grammatical aspect noted by none of these scholars is that the plural πληρωθῶσιν (*plerothosin*) agrees with the plural αἱ γραφαί (*ai graphai*), "the Scriptures."[84] As the standard citation for a passage uses the singular πληρωθῇ (*plerothe*), the use of the plural in this verse suggests that Jesus was citing multiple Scriptures simultaneously to provide a harmony of witness regarding the events of His arrest, trial, and execution.

---

80 Timothy J. Geddert, *Believers Church Bible Commentary: Mark* (Scottdale, PA: Herald, 2001), 353.

81 Schnabel, *Mark*, 365.

82 Stein, *Mark*, 673.

83 Jarvis and Johnson, *Mark*, 481.

84 BDAG, s.v., "γραφή," 1:206.

Because of this grammatical feature, it is not necessary to postulate as the commentators have that Jesus is referencing one Scripture and one only, or to debate which Scripture is the one and only best fit as does Stein.[85] The best view for accommodating the plural verb and accompanying plural recipient of the verbal action is a hybrid of Jarvis and Johnson's with that of Stein, viewing Isaiah 53:12 and Zechariah 13:7 both as passages referenced in this citation by Jesus, though He could have been referring to more verses than even these. Such a view is visible in the work of Heil, who does not attempt to tie the citation by Jesus to any one verse but instead notes that the work of the crowd that arrested Jesus accomplished God's plan as laid out in the Tanach.[86]

Although it cannot be said with absolute certainty which Scriptures Jesus had on His mind in Mark 14:49, the existence of specific predictive passages appropriate to the context of this utterance by Jesus suggests that πληρωθῶσιν (*plerothosin*) carries a destructive sense in this verse, in accordance with its use to describe the occurrence of a previously predicted event. As such, the best gloss for the verb in this case is "be fulfilled, come to pass." As is also the case with the other uses of πληρόω (*pleroo*) forms in citational and allusional formulae, the formulaic use in this passage significantly hinders its usefulness for interpreting Matthew 5:17.

The Gospel of Matthew (Excluding 5:17)

The uses of πληρόω (*pleroo*) in Matthew may be understood as a central theme of the Gospel, due to the frequent use of this verb at key points throughout the narrative. This verb even appears in the first instance of direct discourse from Jesus in Matthew 3:15.[87] Given the significant

---

85 Stein, *Mark*, 673.

86 John Paul Heil, "Mark 14:1-52: Narrative Structure and Reader-Response", *Bib* 71, no. 3 (1990): 328.

87 Matteo Munari, "Fulfilling Every Act of Righteousness (Matt. 3:15)," *LASBF* 66

thematic implications of πληρόω (*pleroo*) in Matthew, and since the key verse under scrutiny in this study is Jesus' discourse in Matthew 5:17, the five other occasions where Jesus uses the verb in this Gospel are perhaps the most relevant for clarifying its meaning in that passage. This is especially the case because, while several of the other Gospels, notably Mark and John, feature a heavy concentration of passive forms of πληρόω (*pleroo*) within their recorded discourses of Jesus, in Matthew the speech of Jesus uses active forms of the verb most of the time, and it is the three uses outside of Matthew 5:17 where active forms of the verb appear that are of greatest interest to the interpretation of this key verse.

1. To Perform the Greatest of All Righteous Deeds: Matthew 3:15

> ἀποκριθεὶς δὲ ὁ Ἰησοῦς εἶπεν ⸀πρὸς αὐτόν⸋· ἄφες ἄρτι, οὕτως γὰρ πρέπον ἐστὶν ἡμῖν **πληρῶσαι** πᾶσαν δικαιοσύνην. τότε ἀφίησιν αὐτόν ⸆. (NA28)
>
> "But Jesus answering him said to him, 'Permit it now, for thus it is fitting for us **to perform** the greatest righteousness.' Then he consented." (Author's Translation)

This passage represents a unique and highly debated use of πληρόω (*pleroo*) due to the direct object and recipient of the verbal action δικαιοσύνην (pronounced *dee-kai-ah-soon-en*, transliterated *dikaiosunen*).[88] This noun, usually translated "righteousness," makes interpretation of the use of πληρόω (*pleroo*) difficult in this case because most of the normal uses of πληρόω (*pleroo*) do not fit well with the

(2016): 69.

88 Munari, "Act of Righteousness," 70.

noun.[89] Blomberg[90] and Osborne[91] understand πᾶσαν δικαιοσύνην (*pasan dikaiosunen*) to refer to everything required for right standing with God, and gloss πληρόω (*pleroo*) as "complete," viewing the baptism of Jesus as the consummate act that made Him obedient to God's will. Quarles notes that the grammatical emphasis of the sentence is on the individual righteous acts and not the totality of right standing.[92] Munari proposes that δικαιοσύνην (*dikaiosunen*) represents the will of God, and the accompanying verb represents both Christ's and John's submission to that will.[93]

In the end, Quarles' view on the meaning of δικαιοσύνην (*dikaiosunen*) offers the best explanation of this word and clarification on the meaning of πληρόω (*pleroo*). This is because the emphasis on individual righteous acts noted by Quarles squares well with one of the possible lexical emphases for πληρόω (*pleroo*), the emphasis on an event or individual representing the ultimate or consummate representation of a type.[94] This use of πληρόω (*pleroo*) is attested in John 13:18, where Judas is listed as the consummate example of a treacherous friend, a fact noted in the preceding commentary on that verse. Assuming a similar emphasis for πληρόω (*pleroo*) here, the verb would carry a gloss of "perform" or "accomplish" and would have a constructive meaning that could be interpretively rendered in its phrase as "to accomplish the crown of all righteous acts" (Matthew 3:15).

Understanding this verse is very significant for the interpretation of

---

89 Munari, "Act of Righteousness." 69.
90 Blomberg, *Matthew*, 67.
91 Osborne, Matthew, 122.
92 Quarles, *Matthew*, 37.
93 Munari, "Act of Righteousness," 77.
94 For a more detailed survey of the use of πληρόω in a sense of consummation or culmination, specifically in the Gospel of John, see Christopher Cone, "Parallelism of Foreshadowing and Fulfillment: Considering Affinity and Dissimilarity in Johannine and Matthean Use of Old Testament Prophecy," *JMT* 23, no. 1 (2019): 42–55.

Matthew 5:17 because the two passages are located spatially close to one another, both have an abstract recipient of the verbal action for πληρόω (*pleroo*), and both use the same inflected form of the verb, the aorist active infinitive. As such, this verse is highly relevant for Matthew 5:17, and being a constructive use presents an equal and opposite contextual passage to Luke 24:44. Because of this, any argument that the use of πληρόω (*pleroo*) in Matthew 5:17 is destructive must answer why this verse would have a different use.

2. When the Net Was Filled: Matthew 13:48

> ⸀ἣν ὅτε⸌ **ἐπληρώθη** ⸀ἀναβιβάσαντες ἐπὶ τὸν αἰγιαλὸν καὶ καθίσαντες συνέλεξαν τὰ ⸀καλὰ εἰς ⸀1ἄγγη, τὰ δὲ σαπρὰ ἔξω ἔβαλον. (NA28)
>
> ...which when it **was full** they brought it up on shore and sitting down, they gathered the good fish into containers, but the bad fish they threw out. (Author's Translation)

This passage represents the only use of πληρόω (*pleroo*) with a concrete recipient of the verbal action, namely σαγήνη (*sagene*), "net," in the book of Matthew.[95] Not surprisingly, this passage is a part of Jesus' parable of the net, a member of the collection of parables which takes up a significant portion of Matthew 13. As a singular example within Matthew, this use of πληρόω (*pleroo*) also carries the meaning closest to the basic meaning of the verb, the sense of filling to capacity. Although a net is a unique type of container the level of abstraction involved is minimal, and as such it is easy to determine that this use is constructive, with a gloss of "filled."

95 Munari, "Act of Righteousness," 70.

In this respect, Osborne[96] and Blomberg[97] affirm such an interpretation, while Turner,[98] Quarles,[99] and Allen[100] gloss over the verb's meaning, apparently considering it to be sufficiently obvious as to need no further comment. Davies and Allison only state that this use of πληρόω (*pleroo*) lacks theological content, while noting that some wish to read a sense of consummation into the verb.[101] While the tense and mood of the verb here are the same as in Matthew 5:17, the inflected form here is passive, marking the only use of the passive of πληρόω (*pleroo*) in Matthew that is not in a formula citation.[102] This, along with the concrete recipient of the verbal action, limits the relevance of this verse for application to Matthew 5:17.

3. Fill the Measure of Your Fathers: Matthew 23:32

> "καὶ ὑμεῖς ⸀**πληρώσατε** τὸ μέτρον τῶν πατέρων ὑμῶν." (NA28)

> "And you all **must fill up** the measure of your fathers." (Author's Translation)

This use of πληρόω (*pleroo*) in Jesus' condemnation of the Pharisees is technically abstract, since the implied indirect object is deeds instead of a physical substance. However, the vocabulary of the verse forms a stout metaphorical connection to the concrete meaning of πληρόω (*pleroo*)

---

96 Grant R. Osborne, *Matthew*, ECNT (Grand Rapids, MI: Zondervan, 2010), 574.
97 Blomberg, *Matthew*, 193.
98 David L Turner, *Matthew*, BECNT (Grand Rapids, MI: Baker Academic, 2008), 353.
99 Quarles, *Matthew*, 155-156.
100 Allen, *St. Matthew*, 2004.
101 W.D. Davies and Dale C. Allison Jr., *A Critical and Exegetical Commentary on the Gospel According to Saint Matthew: Matthew 8-18, Volume II*, ICC (Edinburgh: T&T Clark, 1991), 441.
102 Munari, "Act of Righteousness," 70.

with the recipient of the verbal action μέτρον (*metron*), "measure."[103] The use of this term creates a mental image that relates to the concrete meaning of πληρόω (*pleroo*), as noted by Osborne[104] and Quarles.[105] This concrete image clarifies the abstract meaning in view for this passage, which is that Jesus is commanding the Pharisees to treat Him the same way their ancestors treated the prophets.[106]

Although the primary emphasis of this passage is on the behavior of the Pharisees, and thus on the one hand is focused on them behaving in accordance with the deeds of their ancestors, the fact that Jesus is the victim of their rejection and ill-treatment adds a consummate element to this use of πληρόω (*pleroo*) that is similar to Matthew 3:15, John 13:18, and John 15:25, marking the Pharisees as the ultimate example of the murderous attitude of their ancestors.[107] Based on these things, this use of πληρόω (*pleroo*) is constructive, and the best gloss to make the metaphor of the passage clear is "fill." Although the concrete metaphor and imperative mood are different from Matthew 5:17, both forms of πληρόω (*pleroo*) are aorist in tense and active in mood, which gives this passage some relevance for interpreting Matthew 5:17.

4. How Will the Scriptures be Fulfilled?: Matthew 26:54

> πῶς οὖν **πληρωθῶσιν** αἱ γραφαὶ ὅτι οὕτως δεῖ γενέσθαι; (NA28)
>
> "How then will the writings **be accomplished** that show it must be this way?" (Author's Translation)

---

103 BDAG, s.v., "μέτρον," 1:644.
104 Osborne, *Matthew*, 917.
105 Quarles, *Matthew*, 276.
106 See Turner, *Matthew*, 557–558; Blomberg, *Matthew*, 301.
107 Turner, *Matthew*, 558.

This verse together with Matthew 26:56 represent the only occasion in Matthew where Jesus uses citation formulae in His direct discourse. Although there is no reference to a specific passage of Scripture, the phrase ὅτι οὕτως δεῖ γενέσθαι (transliterated *hoti outos dei genesthai*), "that it is necessary to happen" (Matthew 26:54, Author's translation), suggests that specific prophecies are in mind. Although one example of prophecy that comes to mind is Isaiah 53, the commentators generally do not attempt to identify a specific passage cited, likely a wise path since as shown in Mark 14:49 there are times when Jesus references multiple Scriptures in a single citation.

Further, the commentators generally do not elaborate on the meaning of πληρόω (*pleroo*) in this verse, instead operating on the assumption that the meaning is destructive with a gloss of "fulfill, come to pass." Osborne,[108] Quarles,[109] and Turner[110] all express this view, while Blomberg[111] does not comment on the πληρόω (*pleroo*) form. Given the similarities of this passage to Mark 14:49 in that this passage represents a citation of multiple specific Scriptures that are implied only through a discussion of their message, the consensus view is the strongest interpretation of the use of πληρόω (*pleroo*) here. As such, Matthew 26:54 represents the only destructive use of πληρόω (*pleroo*) in the Matthean discourses of Jesus, though the formulaic use and passive inflection reduce its relevance for Matthew 5:17.

5. So it Might Fulfill the Writings of the Prophets: Matthew 26:56

> τοῦτο δὲ ὅλον γέγονεν ἵνα **πληρωθῶσιν** αἱ γραφαὶ τῶν προφητῶν. Τότε οἱ μαθηταὶ ⸆ πάντες ἀφέντες αὐτὸν ἔφυγον. (NA28)

---

108 Osborne, *Matthew*, 1060.
109 Quarles, *Matthew*, 323.
110 Turner, *Matthew*, 637.
111 Blomberg, *Matthew*, 345.

> "But this whole thing happened so that it might **accomplish** the writings of the prophets." Then the disciples all abandoned Him and fled. (Author's Translation)

Like Mark 14:49 and John 17:12, there is no indication of a particular Scripture being in view, but rather Yeshua is echoing the general message of the Tanach concerning the events that have in that moment just transpired. The commentators generally agree on this point, though Blomberg,[112] Osborne,[113] and Turner[114] maintain that the whole Tanach is in view, while Quarles suggests on grammatical grounds that only the Prophets might be in view.[115] However, the difference between these points of view does not affect the meaning of πληρόω (*pleroo*), for all agree that it is used in the standard formulaic sense of marking an allusion to the Tanach. As such, in the absence of a reference to specific predictive passages, this is a hybrid use of πληρόω (*pleroo*) that may be glossed "be fulfilled, come to pass." Given that this passage represents the same use, and even the same inflected form, as Mark 14:49, its relevance for Matthew 5:17 is greatly limited.

112 Blomberg, *Matthew*, 345.
113 Osborne, *Matthew*, 1061.
114 Turner, *Matthew*, 637.
115 Quarles, *Matthew*, 324.

Chapter 4

Putting it All Together

In the survey of passages from the previous chapter, one use of πληρόω (*pleroo*) by Jesus has been extensively mentioned but not yet given full treatment: Matthew 5:17. The delay in analyzing this verse was purposeful, for the interpretation of this verse is the most central to the question and debate this book seeks to answer. As such, up to this point it has been necessary to gather and analyze as much relevant data as possible, primarily from Yeshua's other uses of πληρόω (*pleroo*) throughout the Gospels, but also from the broader Apostolic Writings, the Septuagint, and other ancient literature, in order to bring the full witness of this evidence to bear on defining the πληρόω (*pleroo*) form in Matthew 5:17. Now that this has been completed, it is possible to analyze Matthew 5:17 in light of its full grammatical, historical, and discourse contexts, which will be the central focus of this chapter.

I Came Not to Destroy but to Perform: Matthew 5:17

> Μὴ νομίσητε ὅτι ἦλθον καταλῦσαι τὸν νόμον ἢ τοὺς προφήτας· οὐκ ἦλθον καταλῦσαι ἀλλὰ **πληρῶσαι**. (NA28)
>
> Do not even think that I came to destroy the Law or the Prophets; I came not to destroy but **to perform** their consummate words. (Author's Translation)

As observed throughout the case studies on πληρόω (*pleroo*), one of the most helpful indicators for identifying the use of a particular form of πληρόω (*pleroo*) in its context is the recipient of the verbal action. Typically, a tangible and impersonal recipient indicates a concrete and constructive use of the verb.[1] Tangible and personal recipients, on the other hand, tend to indicate an abstract and constructive use that often can be related to a tangible use by metaphor.[2] Most intangible recipients indicate an abstract use that can be either constructive or destructive, but when Scripture is the recipient, a hybrid use of πληρόω (*pleroo*) is frequently in view.[3]

Recipient of Verbal Action

In Matthew 5:17, the recipient of the verbal action of πληρόω (*pleroo*) is τὸν νόμον ἢ τοὺς προφήτας (NA28) (transliterated *ton nomon he tous prophetas*), "the Law and the Prophets" (Author's translation), which is a way of referring to the Tanach.[4] At first glance this appears to confirm a hybrid meaning for πληρῶσαι (*plerosai*), but this passage lacks one key element necessary to confirm a hybrid use, namely the citation of or allusion to a specific passage of Scripture. While the context by itself makes it clear that Jesus is not making a citation or allusion, there is also grammatical evidence in this regard. Quarles notes the use of the disjunctive particle ἢ (*he*) linking τὸν νόμον (*ton nomon*) with τοὺς προφήτας (*tous prophetas*) where the conjunction καὶ (*kai*) would be used if this verse corresponded to a citation.[5]

The particle chosen is not the only dissimilarity between Matthew 5:17 and the citation formulaic use of πληρόω (*pleroo*). Citations with a hybrid use of πληρόω (*pleroo*) generally use a passive and not an active form of the verb like the one found in Matthew 5:17.[6] Further, a citation formula nearly always incorporates a form of λέγω (*lego*), γράφω

1 See Genesis 1:22 (LXX); Matthew 13:48; *Shepherd of Hermas* 84:5.

2 See 1 Kingdoms 7:2 (LXX), Acts 13:52, Romans 15:3.

3 See 2 Chronicles 26:21, John 15:11. For Hybrid citations of Scripture see Matthew 26:56, John 12:38.

4 Osborne, *Matthew*, 187.

5 Quarles, *Matthew*, 54.

6 Hegg, *Matthew: Volume 1*, 173.

(*grapho*), or γραφή (*graphe*) before the cited material, though sometimes the cited material is only implied, as in John 17:12.[7] Forms of λέγω (*lego*), γράφω (*grapho*), or γραφή (*graphe*) do not appear in Matthew 5:17, which makes it unlikely that a citational use is in mind for πληρῶσαι (*plerosai*) here, and makes it possible that a constructive or destructive meaning is in view.

In this respect, there are only a few other times in the Gospels where Jesus uses a form of πληρόω (*pleroo*) with a similar inflected form and a similar recipient of the verbal action where a citation of Scripture is not in view, and these are Matthew 3:15, Luke 4:21, Luke 22:16, Luke 24:44, John 16:6, John 16:24, and John 17:13. While constructive, hybrid, and destructive uses of πληρόω (*pleroo*) are all represented among these verses, the most relevant are Matthew 3:15, with its constructive use of πληρόω (*pleroo*), and Luke 24:44, with its destructive use. Although a conclusion that aligns Matthew 5:17 with either of these passages will have to explain why the other is less relevant, taking the use of πληρῶσαι (*plerosai*) in Matthew 5:17 as hybrid would have to contend with both passages. On these grounds, it appears most likely that πληρῶσαι (*plerosai*) in Matthew 5:17 is either constructive or destructive, and likely not hybrid.

General Observations on πληρόω in Jesus' Discourses

Stepping back to assess the statistical information regarding Yeshua's use of πληρόω (*pleroo*) from chapter 3, all three categories of use appear with nearly equal frequency in the discourses of Jesus. The constructive uses are most common by the slimmest margin at seven occurrences, while the hybrid and destructive uses occur with equal frequency at six uses each.[8]

---

7 *TNDT*, 1:868.

8 Constructive uses are Matthew 3:15, 13:48, 23:32, Luke 22:16, John 13:18, 15:11, 16:6. Hybrid uses are Matthew 26:56, Luke 4:21, John 15:25, 16:24, 17:12, 17:13. Destructive uses are Matthew 26:54, Mark 1:15, 14:49, Luke 21:24, 24:44, John 7:8.

This contrasts with the general trends of πληρόω (*pleroo*) usage in other ancient literature, for outside the discourses of Jesus constructive uses are the most common for πληρόω (*pleroo*) by a significant margin, as studied in chapter two. What is more, there are other differences that may be noted between the statistics of Christ's uses of πληρόω (*pleroo*) and uses of the term in secular ancient literature.

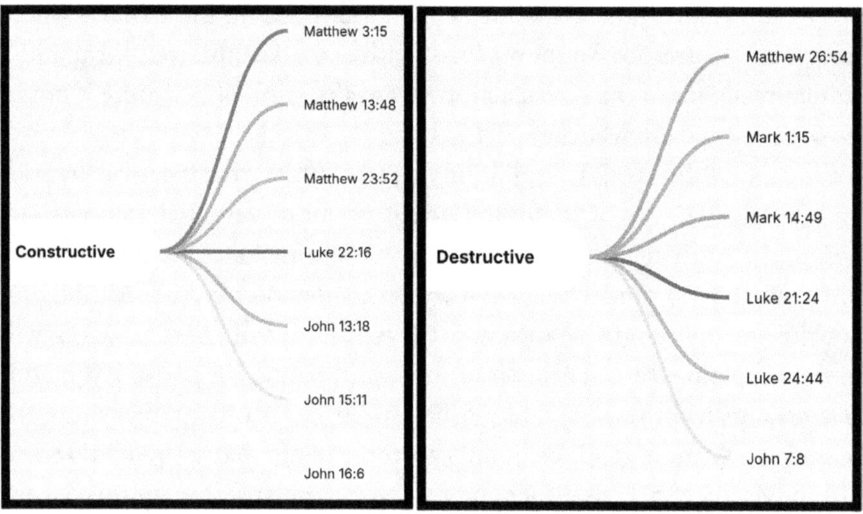

Figure 2: Constructive uses of πληρόω (*pleroo.*)

Figure 3: Destructive uses of πληρόω (*pleroo.*)

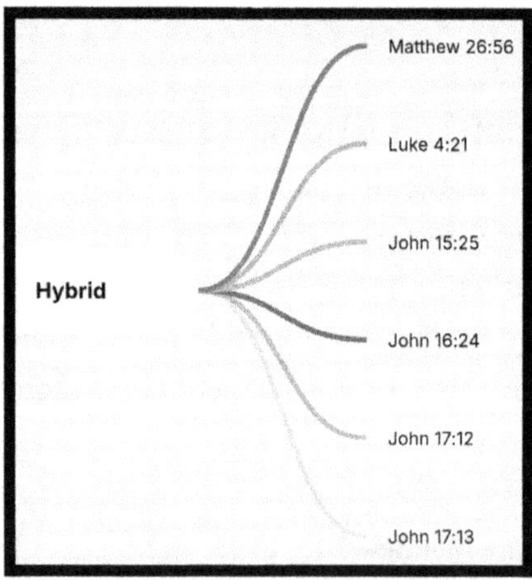

Figure 4: Hybrid uses of πληρόω (*pleroo.*)

Most immediately apparent is that, although in both cases the constructive uses of πληρόω (*pleroo*) outnumber the destructive, constructive uses have a far smaller lead in Jesus' discourses, at roughly one in three uses in comparison to the four out of every five uses seen in secular literature. Correspondingly, Jesus' discourses use destructive forms of πληρόω (*pleroo*) more frequently than other ancient literature, at one out of three instead of one out of five uses. The remaining third of the uses of πληρόω (*pleroo*) by Yeshua are hybrid, which is a use not extensively attested in secular literature. This fact may be accounted for by observing that many of the hybrid uses of πληρόω (*pleroo*) are citations and allusions to Scriptural texts and prophecies, citations and allusions that secular Koine Greek literature would not often make.[9] Taken statistically, this information suggests that none of the three possible interpretations for πληρόω (*pleroo*) in Matthew 5:17 should be immediately discounted, as even those uses that are rare in literature outside the Bible are attested in discourses of Yeshua.

Although this statistical analysis is helpful for clarifying general trends in the use of πληρόω (*pleroo*) within the discourses of Yeshua, a study that will prove more directly relevant to answering the specific use in Matthew 5:17 is one directed toward the two passages that have been shown to have the greatest relevance for Matthew 5:17. In this respect, the next logical step is to review the evidence in favor of taking one passage or the other as the best controlling context for interpreting Matthew 5:17, because this evidence will be the most important for the final determination. Each passage will be analyzed in the same order that they were reviewed in Chapter 3, with Luke 24:44 first and Matthew 3:15 second.

---

9 In the discourses of Jesus, four of the six Hybrid uses of πληρόω make reference to Scripture in the style of a citation formula: Matthew 26:56, Luke 4:21, John 15:25, and John 17:12.

Luke 24:44 and Matthew 3:15

In the passage from Luke, the recipient of the verbal action is the Scriptures, and the reference is expressed more fully than in Matthew 5:17, including the Psalms as a metonym for the Writings in addition to the Law and the Prophets. Taking each verse in isolation, it appears that Luke 24:44 is preferable because the recipient of the verbal action in Matthew 3:15 is different, even if it is also abstract. However, Luke 24:46 reveals that the Luke 24:44 reference is specific to the *predictive prophecies* in the OT.[10] This emphasis is absent in the context of Matthew 5:17. If there is any emphasis in that context, it is toward the moral commands of the OT rather than the predictive prophecies.[11] Thus, while the recipient of the verbal action in Luke 24:44 more closely resembles that of Matthew 5:17 than does the recipient in Matthew 3:15, neither passage corresponds perfectly to Matthew 5:17.

In Matthew 3:15, several factors offer a favorable comparison to Matthew 5:17. Both texts are from the same Gospel and are separated by only a few chapters, which increases the likelihood that the author would consciously use a similar meaning.[12] A stronger piece of evidence is that the inflected forms of Matthew 3:15 and Matthew 5:17 are identical, with the Aorist Active Infinitive πληρῶσαι (*plerosai*) used in both verses. While the inflected form of Luke 24:44 is similar in that it is an Aorist Infinitive, the Luke passage uses the Passive πληρωθῆναι (*plerothenai*). This is a relevant difference because, as noted in Chapter 1, the Active forms of πληρόω (*pleroo*) are not used in the citation formulae of the Gospels, the most similar group of uses to Luke 24:44. Thus, in this respect the Luke passage is distanced from Matthew 5:17 in terms of relevance.

10 Garland, *Luke*, 1008.
11 Turner, *Matthew*, 162.
12 Duvall and Hays, *God's Word*, 154.

The Immediate Context of Matthew 5:17

While the matters discussed up to this point may lean toward the conclusion that Matthew 3:15 is generally the favorable context for interpreting Matthew 5:17, the evidence is not strong enough to dismiss the relevance of Luke 24:44. In this respect there is another area of evidence that provides additional support for the interpretation of πληρῶσαι (*plerosai*): the grammatical structure of Matthew 5:17 and the verses in its immediate context. The most immediate factor relevant for the meaning of πληρῶσαι (*plerosai*) is its contrast with καταλῦσαι (*katalusai*), another Aorist Active Infinitive, which may be glossed "destroy, put an end to."[13] As noted by Osborne, Christ offers a comparison between πληρῶσαι (*plerosai*) and καταλῦσαι (*katalusai*) as though they carry opposite meanings in this context.[14] This provides a test as to whether Matthew 3:15 or Luke 24:44 is the better controlling context for Matthew 5:17. The test is which use of πληρόω (*pleroo*) contrasts with the meaning of the καταλύω (*kataluo*) form in Matthew 5:17.

Fortunately, the precise import of καταλῦσαι (*katalusai*) is easy to determine, as the next verse of Yeshua's discourse expounds on the meaning of this verb by saying, "...until heaven and earth pass away, not the smallest letter or stroke shall pass from the Law until all is accomplished" (Matthew 5:18, NASB95). While many commentators focus on the temporal phrases of verse 18, it is also important to note that this verse clarifies the meaning of καταλῦσαι (*katalusai*), showing that in the preceding verse Yeshua states His intent is not to erase even a single letter of Scripture as it stood in His day.[15] Verse 19 further confirms the sense of καταλῦσαι (*katalusai*) by the words Yeshua speaks against the person who may "loosen," λύσῃ (pronounced *loo-say*, transliterated *luse*), the commands of the Scriptures.[16]

---

13 BDAG, s.v., "καταλύω," 1:521.
14 Osborne, *Matthew*, 187.
15 Osborne, *Matthew*, 187.
16 Quarles, *Matthew*, 54.

Based on this context, καταλῦσαι (*katalusai*) refers not just to the wholesale rejection of the Scriptures but also to the reduction of their relevance for believers in the age of Christ, conveying what this study has termed a *destructive* meaning.[17] The use of πληρωθῆναι (*plerothenai*) in Luke 24:44 carries a complimentary meaning to this, and if such a destructive use of πληρόω (*pleroo*) is applied to Matthew 5:17, the clause may be interpretively translated as: "I did not come to bring the Law or the Prophets to a close, but to accomplish their closure." This translation makes it apparent that the meaning of πληρωθῆναι (*plerothenai*) in Luke 24:44 is so close to καταλῦσαι (*katalusai*) in Matthew 5:17 that the intended contrast in the sentence structure collapses. When the meaning of πληρωθῆναι (*plerothenai*) from the Luke passage is applied to πληρῶσαι (*plerosai*) in Matthew 5:17, the antithesis with καταλῦσαι (*katalusai*) does not make sense.

In contrast, the use of πληρῶσαι (*plerosai*) in Matthew 3:15 forms a strong contrast in meaning with καταλῦσαι (*katalusai*) in Matthew 5:17. Adopting the meaning from Matthew 3:15 for πληρῶσαι (*plerosai*) in Matthew 5:17 results in the interpretive translation of "I did not come to bring the Law or the Prophets to a close, but to perform their consummate words" (Matthew 5:17). This constructive meaning for πληρῶσαι (*plerosai*) fits the contrastive structure of the sentence very well. As such, the meaning of πληρῶσαι (*plerosai*) in Matthew 3:15 makes good sense when applied to the same verb's use in Matthew 5:17.

This assessment's accuracy is confirmed by other features in the discourse surrounding Matthew 5:17. As Wilber notes in his assessment of Matthew 5:17–20, verse 19 illustrates a flow of thought parallel to that of verse 17 in saying, "...whoever loosens one of the least of these commandments and teaches people in this way, he will be called least... but whoever does and teaches [the commandments] will be called great..." (Matthew 5:19, Author's Translation). In this verse, Wilber rightly

17 Turner, *Matthew*, 163.

notes that λύση (*lu-say*, "loosen," transliterated *luse*) and ποιήση (*poi-ay-say*, "do," transliterated *poiese*) in verse 19 carry meanings parallel to καταλῦσαι (*katalusai*) and πληρῶσαι (*plerosai*) in verse 17. Specifically, λύση (*luse*) and καταλῦσαι (*katalusai*) both refer to a reduction of the Torah's relevance for followers of Yeshua, whereas ποιήση (*poiese*) and πληρῶσαι (*plerosai*) carry the opposite meaning, emphasizing the preservation and deepening of the Torah's relevance for the Church.[18] This parallel structure with different vocabulary reinforces the notion that both verses 17 and 19 have a contrastive structure, making an extremely strong case that Matthew 3:15 rather than Luke 24:44 is the best passage to use as a guide for interpreting Matthew 5:17, favoring a pronomian interpretation.

Supplementary Evidence

Having assessed the two passages of greatest relevance for the interpretation of Matthew 5:17, it is now proper to return to the remaining passages mentioned previously as having relevance worthy of note for Matthew 5:17, namely Luke 4:21, Luke 22:16, John 16:6, John 16:24, and John 17:13. With respect to these other passages, the first general trend visible in the group is that none have a purely destructive meaning, although John 16:24 and 17:13 are hybrid uses of πληρόω (*pleroo*) with slight destructive emphasis. This fits well with the observation made previously that the destructive use of πληρόω (*pleroo*) in Matthew 5:17 is the least likely of all options due to the contrast with the pair of καταλύω (*kataluo*) forms in the sentence. However, the fact that Luke 4:21, John 16:24, and John 17:13 are hybrid increases the burden of proof for those who view the πληρόω (*pleroo*) form in Matthew 5:17 as constructive similar to Matthew 3:15. Such a view must provide a substantive explanation of why Matthew

18 David Wilber, *How Jesus Fulfilled the Law: A pronomian Pocket Guide to Matthew 5:17–20* (Clover, SC: Pronomian Publishing, 2024), 28.

5:17 is not a hybrid use. After all, a hybrid use of πληρόω (*pleroo*) would provide enough contrast with καταλύω (*kataluo*) to make grammatical sense and yet could avoid the ramifications of a constructive meaning for Christian orthopraxy.[19]

As noted previously, two pieces of evidence that weigh against a hybrid interpretation for πληρόω (*pleroo*) are the fact that Matthew 5:17 does not represent a citation, and that the two passages of greatest relevance for this verse do not contain a hybrid use of πληρόω (*pleroo*). Thus, the best answer to the question of whether a hybrid interpretation is appropriate in Matthew 5:17 will come from the analysis of the three verses previously noted as relevant hybrid uses of πληρόω (*pleroo*) to see if these possess sufficiently similar features to outweigh the testimony of Matthew 3:15 and Luke 24:44. While Luke 4:21 contains a similar recipient of the verbal action to Matthew 5:17, both verses from John have χαρὰ (*chara*), "joy," as the recipient of the verbal action.[20] One area where all three verses differ from Matthew 5:17 is that they use passive forms of πληρόω (*pleroo*) and are in the perfect tense. The form in Luke 4:21 is in the indicative mood, but both John 16:24 and 17:13 use participle forms of πληρόω (*pleroo*), being like the use in Matthew 5:17 in that they are non-indicative mood.

In these respects, the uses in these three verses each do have at least one key point of similarity but also differ from the use in Matthew 5:17 in ways significant enough that they do not outweigh the similarities between Matthew 3:15 and 5:17. For this reason the support for interpreting the πληρόω (*pleroo*) form in Matthew 5:17 as hybrid in meaning is relatively weak. Such a view is strengthened by the observation that the two remaining verses with relevance for Matthew 5:17, namely Luke 22:16 and John 16:6, are constructive uses of πληρόω (*pleroo*). While both have differences with Matthew 5:17, Luke 22:16 specifically has

---

19 A good example of how this works in practice is Blomberg, *Matthew*, 90.
20 BDAG, s.v., "χαρὰ," 1:1077.

a higher degree of similarity than any of the hybrid passages, given that Luke 22:16 uses a non-indicative form of πληρόω (*pleroo*) along with a thematically similar recipient of the verbal action. As such, Luke 22:16 and John 16:6 serve as an effective counterbalance to the passages with hybrid meanings.

Answer to the Research Question

This information confirms the weight of the other data points, indicating that Matthew 3:15 is a better controlling context than Luke 24:44 when seeking to understand the use of πληρόω (*pleroo*) in Matthew 5:17. Further, such a construct provides a two-fold explanation as to why the meaning of πληρόω (*pleroo*) in Matthew 5:17 is different from Luke 24:44. First, while both verses use πληρόω (*pleroo*) forms in reference to Scripture, the Luke passage speaks of the predictive prophecies in Scripture whereas Matthew speaks of the Scriptures as a whole with focus on the moral demands of God's word, as evidenced in Matthew 5:18 and 19.

Second, the attempt to read πληρῶσαι (*plerosai*) in Matthew 5:17 with as close as possible of a meaning to that given for πληρωθῆναι (*plerothenai*) in the Luke passage resulted in a reading of Matthew 5:17 that affirmed that Jesus' mission involved a reduction of relevance for the Torah in the lives of modern believers while simultaneously denying the same. Given the presence of an interpretation that gives πληρῶσαι (*plerosai*) the expected contrastive import, the poor fit of a destructive meaning for πληρόω (*pleroo*) in the context of Matthew 5:17 signals that such a view, while not completely untenable, is grammatically and logically inferior.[21] As such, taking Matthew 3:15 as the most relevant context for the use of πληρόω (*pleroo*) in Matthew 5:17 presents a strong case that the use is constructive, with a gloss of "perform," "establish," "create," or in an additive sense "complete."

---

21 McKenzie, "Pronomian Paradigm," 61.

Implications of Research

Now that the study is complete, we can see that it has helped fill several key gaps in the existing research regarding the use of πληρόω (*pleroo*) in Matthew 5:17. While the research confirmed the general sentiment of previous scholarship that πληρόω (*pleroo*) in its general usage more frequently carries an additive, constructive sense, it also provides insight into the specific instances where πληρόω (*pleroo*) does carry a destructive meaning, most of which are specialized abstract uses that usually refer to the completion or satisfaction of a limited number of referents. As such, this study suggests that it may be appropriate to view most πληρόω (*pleroo*) forms as constructive unless there is good precedent for a hybrid or destructive use in similar contexts.

Another gap this study filled is accomplishing a proper study of the uses of πληρόω (*pleroo*) within the discourses of Yeshua across all four Gospels. In general survey, the study demonstrated that Yeshua uses the word in a wide variety of contexts, with equally varied meanings. However, His uses of πληρόω (*pleroo*) are like the word's use in later Christian literature in that the word is almost exclusively used abstractly, with only Matthew 13:48 representing a concrete use in the discourses of Yeshua. Although in other literature constructive uses of πληρόω (*pleroo*) tend to be the most basic, the uses of this verb in the discourses of Yeshua break with this pattern, and constructive uses are attested with only slightly greater frequency than are destructive and hybrid uses.

The specific conclusions of the study as they pertain to Matthew 5:17 also have significant ramifications for the debate concerning the relationship between Christ and the Torah, and more broadly the Torah and the Church. The observation that πληρόω (*pleroo*) in Matthew 5:17 is constructive favors the pronomian family of positions. Although this verse alone does not resolve the broader debate, the constructive meaning of πληρόω (*pleroo*) in Matthew 5:17 offers a serious challenge to the notion that any antinomian view is Biblically tenable.

In such respect, the constructive use of πληρόω (*pleroo*) in Matthew

5:17 leads to an interpretation that directly speaks to the role of the Law in the life of the modern Christian. Interpreting Matthew 5:17 in accordance with the manner of this study shows that Christ viewed the Law not as something old or redundant with the coming of His ministry, but rather as the foundation of His life, work, and revelation. As such, the work of Christ does not mark the end of the Law but rather stands as its climactic chapter in the progressive revelation of God. In this function the Gospel does not supersede or replace the Law or the Prophets, but rather compliments them, for both Matthew 5:17 and its surrounding context leave the strong implication that obedience to the commandments of the Torah should in the view of Christ form the foundation of every Christian's approach to living their daily lives.

Final Thoughts and Suggestions for Further Research

As noted in the introduction of this work, the constructive and pronomian interpretation of Matthew 5:17, concluded to be correct by this study, stands at odds with the traditional Christian majority view on orthopraxy. Most Christians throughout the centuries have taught that the work of Christ brought about major changes to the relevance of the Torah for the Church, setting aside the need for Christians to obey such laws as the Biblical feasts, the dietary laws, and other such commandments that might be labeled "civil" or "ceremonial."[22] However, as has been shown, the constructive and pronomian interpretation of Matthew 5:17 is stronger in multiple ways, which opens the possibility that the Church may have taught the abolition or setting aside of these parts of the Torah in error. To confirm the results of the research and realize the full ramifications of Matthew 5:17 for Christian orthopraxy, it is necessary for you to continue searching the Scriptures in areas beyond the scope of the present work.

22 Du Toit, "Dialectical Approach," 50.

Although Matthew 5:17 is a significant text for the relationship between the Christian and the Law, as noted in chapter two, there are many other texts in the Hebrew and Greek Scriptures that speak to the matter. In this respect, the most important step for further research is to compile and study the passages that speak to the Torah's relationship to Christ and the believing community, interpreting each passage responsibly to compile a teaching with the full weight of Biblical witness behind it. Completing this step would provide the foundation to make a more complete comparison of the pronomian and antinomian schools of thought, demonstrating the strengths and weaknesses of each. Perhaps at some point I will publish something along these lines, but even so it would be prudent for you, the reader, to investigate the Scriptures on your own as well.

A thorough investigation of the Bible would provide the volume of information necessary to answer the question of whether a pronomian or antinomian view better suits the overall teaching of Scripture and reveal the most difficult passages that each school of thought must overcome to demonstrate its harmony with the whole of Scripture. It is true that such study could possibly challenge some of the oldest traditions of the Church. However, the detailed exegesis of Matthew 5:17 presented here shows that the issue must be raised and addressed because the strength of the constructive and pronomian interpretation of Matthew 5:17 makes it improper to ignore the possibility that the traditions of majority Christianity may have misunderstood the teachings of Jesus with respect to the relationship of the Law and the Church.

Bibliography

Aland, Barbara, Kurt Aland, Johannes Karavidopoulos, Carlo M. Martini, and Bruce Metzger, Editors. *Novum Testamentum Graece 28th Edition*. Munster, Germany: Deutsche Bibelgesellschaft, 2012.

Allen, Willoughby C. *St. Matthew*. London: T&T Clark International, 2004.

Augustine. *On Christian Doctrine*. In vol. 2 of *The Nicene and Post-Nicene Fathers*, Series 1. Edited by Phillip Schaff. 1886-1889. 14 vols.

_______. *Our Lord's Sermon on the Mount*. In vol. 6 of *The Nicene and Post-Nicene Fathers*, Series 1. Edited by Phillip Schaff. 1886-1889. 14 vols.

Badke, William. *Research Strategies: Finding Your Way Through the Information Fog*. Bloomington, IN: iUniverse, 2017.

Basil. *Letters, Volume I: Letters 1-58*. Translated by Roy J. Deferrari. Loeb Classical Library 190. Cambridge, MA: Harvard University Press, 1926.

Bauer, Walter. *A Greek-English Lexicon of the New Testament and Other Early Christian Literature*. Revised and edited by Frederick W. Danker. 3rd. ed. Chicago: University of Chicago Press, 2000.

Bernard, John Henry. *St. John: Volume 1: 1-7*. London: Bloomsbury T&T Clark, 1999.

Blomberg, Craig L. *Matthew: An Exegetical and Theological Exposition of Holy Scripture*. Nashville, TN: B&H Academic, 1992.

Bock, Darrell L. *Luke*. Grand Rapids, MI: Zondervan, 1996.

Borchert, Gerald L. *John 12-21: An Exegetical and Theological Exposition of Holy Scripture*. Nashville, TN: B&H Academic, 2002.

Bromiley, Geoffrey W. *Theological Dictionary of the New Testament: Abridged in One Volume*. Grand Rapids, MI: William B. Eerdmans.

Burtness, James H. "Life-Style and Law: Some Reflections on Matthew 5:17." *Dialog* 14, no. 1 (Winter 1975): 13-20.

Charry, Ellen T. *Brazos Theological Commentary on the Bible: Psalms 1-50.* Grand Rapids, MI: Brazos, 2015.

Clausen, Marc A. "An Exegetical and Theological Examination of Matthew 5:17-20." Thesis, Liberty University, 1993. Scholars Crossing.

Cone, Christopher. "Parallelism Foreshadowing and Fulfillment: Considering Affinity and Dissimilarity in Johannine and Matthean Use of Old Testament Prophecy." *Journal of Ministry and Theology* 23, no. 1 (2019): 37-57.

Davies, W.D., and Dale C. Allison Jr. *A Critical and Exegetical Commentary on the Gospel According to Saint Matthew: Introduction and Commentary on Matthew I-VII, Volume I.* Edinburgh: T&T Clark, 1988.

———. *A Critical and Exegetical Commentary on the Gospel According to Saint Matthew: Matthew VIII-XVIII, Volume II.* Edinburgh: T&T Clark, 1991.

Diggle, James, B.L. Frasier, Patrick James, O.B. Simkin, A.A. Thompson, and S.J. Westripp. *The Cambridge Greek Lexicon.* Cambridge, United Kingdom: Cambridge University, 2021.

Dillon, Richard J. "Mark 1:1-15: A 'New Evangelization'?" *The Catholic Biblical Quarterly* 76, no. 1 (January 2014): 1-18.

Dummeflow, Rev. J. R., Ed. *A Commentary on the Holy Bible.* New York: MacMillan, 1909.

Du Toit, Philip la Grange. "The Fulfilment of the Law According to Matthew 5:17: A Dialectical Approach." *Acta Theologica* 38, no. 2 (2018): 49-69.

Duvall, J. Scott, and J. Daniel Hays. *Grasping God's Word: A Hands on Approach to Reading, Interpreting, and Applying the Bible.* Grand Rapids, MI: Zondervan Academic, 2020.

Erickson, Millard J. *Christian Theology: Third Edition.* Grand Rapids, MI: Baker Academic, 2013.

Epiphanius. *Against All Heresies.* In Ray A. Pritz, *Nazarene Jewish Christianity: From the End of the New Testament Period Until Its Disappearance in the Fourth Century.* Jerusalem: Magnes Press, 1988.

Eusebius. *Ecclesiastical History, Volume I: Books 1-5.* Translated by Kirsopp Lake. Loeb Classical Library 153. Cambridge, MA: Harvard University Press, 1926.

Galen. *Hygiene, Volume I: Books 1–4.* Edited and translated by Ian Johnston. Loeb Classical Library 535. Cambridge, MA: Harvard University Press, 2018.

Garland, David E. *Exegetical Commentary on the New Testament: Luke.* Grand Rapids, MI: Zondervan, 2011.

Geddert, Timothy J. *Believers Church Bible Commentary: Mark.* Scottdale, PA: Herald, 2001.

Harris, Murray J. *Exegetical Guide to the Greek New Testament: John.* Nashville, TN: B&H Academic, 2015.

Hegg, Tim. *Commentary on the Gospel of Matthew: Volume 1.* Tacoma, WA: TorahResource, 2007.

———. *It Is Often Said: Vol. 4.* Tacoma, WA: TorahResource, 2013.

Heil, John Paul. "Mark 14:1-52: Narrative Structure and Reader-Response." *Biblica* 71, no. 3 (1990): 305-332.

Hera, Marianus Pale. "Christology and Discipleship in John 17." PhD diss., Catholic University of America, 2012. ProQuest (AAT 3544251).

Jarvis, Cynthia A., and E. Elizabeth Johnson, *Feasting on the Gospels: Mark.* Louisville, KY: Westminster John Knox, 2014.

Johnson, Luke Timothy. *Sacra Pagina: The Gospel of Luke.* Collegeville, MN: Liturgical, 1991.

Josephus. *Jewish Antiquities, Volume I: Books 1-3.* Translated by H. St. J. Thackeray. Loeb Classical Library 242. Cambridge, MA: Harvard University Press, 1930.

Kaiser, Walter C. Jr., and Moises Silva. *Introduction to Biblical Hermeneutics.* Grand Rapids, MI: Zondervan Academic, 2007.

Kirk, J.R. Daniel. "Conceptualising Fulfillment in Matthew." *Tyndale Bulletin* 59, no. 1 (2008): 77-98.

Klein, William W., Craig L. Blomberg, and Robert L. Hubbard Jr. *Introduction to Biblical Interpretation.* Grand Rapids, MI: Zondervan, 2017.

Klink, Edward W. *Exegetical Commentary on the New Testament: John.* Grand Rapids, MI: Zondervan, 2016.

Koehler, Ludwig, and Walter Baumgartner. *The Hebrew and Aramaic Lexicon of the Old Testament.* Leiden, Netherlands: Koninklijke Brill NV, 2000.

Lawrence, Arren Bennet. *Comparative Characterization in the Sermon on the Mount: Characterization of the Ideal Disciple.* Eugene, OR: Wipf & Stock, 2017.

Liefeld, Walter L., and David W. Pao. *The Expositor's Bible Commentary: Luke.* Grand Rapids, MI: Zondervan, 2007.

Lisle, Dr. Jason. *The Ultimate Proof of Creation.* Green Forest, AR: Master, 2009.

Louw, Johannes P., and Eugene A. Nida, eds. *Greek-English Lexicon of the New Testament Based on Semantic Domains.* 2nd Ed. New York: United Bible Societies, 1996.

Martyr, Justin. *Dialogue with Trypho the Jew.* Migne, Jaques-Paul, ed. Patrologia graeca. 161 vols. Paris: Migne: 1857-1886.

McKenzie, Gregory Scott, "Pronomian Paradigm: A Pro-Torah, Christocentric Method of Theology and Apologetics" (2024). *Doctoral Dissertations and Projects.* 5623.

https://digitalcommons.liberty.edu/doctoral/5623.

Montanari, Franco, Ivan Garofalo, Daniela Manetti, Madeleine Goh, Chad Matthew Schroeder, Gregory Nagy, Leonard Muellner, Rachel Barritt-Costa, and Center for Hellenic Studies. *The Brill Dictionary of Ancient Greek.* Edited by Madeleine Goh, Chad Matthew Schroeder,

Gregory Nagy, and Leonard Muellner. Translated by Rachel Barritt-Costa. Second printing with corrections. Leiden: Brill, 2018.

Munari, Matteo. "Fulfilling Every Act of Righteousness (Matt 3:15)." *Liber Annuus* 66 (2016): 69-79.

Muraoka, Takamitsu. *A Greek-English Lexicon of the Septuagint*. Leuven: Peeters, 2009.

Oddeng, Zulkifli. "Pleromacy: When Jesus Interpreted the Law and the Prophets." *Studium Biblicum* 1, no. 1 (2024): 52-63.

Osborne, Grant R. *Exegetical Commentary on the New Testament: Matthew*. Grand Rapids, MI: Zondervan, 2010.

Perrin, Nicholas. *Luke: An Introduction and Commentary*. Downers Grove, IL: InterVarsity, 2022.

Pritz, Ray A. *Nazarene Jewish Christianity: From the End of the New Testament Period Until Its Disappearance in the Fourth Century*. Jerusalem: Magnes Press, 1988.

Quarles, Charles L. *Exegetical Guide to the Greek New Testament: Matthew*. Nashville, TN: B&H Academic, 2017.

Schnabel, Ekhard J. *Mark: An Introduction and Commentary*. Downers Grove, IL: InterVarsity, 2015.

Schreiner, Thomas R. *Exegetical Commentary on the New Testament: Galatians*. Grand Rapids, MI: Zondervan Academic, 2010.

———, Luke Timothy Johnson, Douglas A. Campbell and Mark D. Nanos. *Four Views on the Apostle Paul.* Grand Rapids, MI: Zondervan, 2012.

Select Papyri, Volume II: Public Documents. Translated by A. S. Hunt, C. C. Edgar. Loeb Classical Library 282. Cambridge, MA: Harvard University Press, 1934. Sewakpo, Honore. "Jesus' Fulfillment of the Law in Mathew 5:17: A Panacea for Breaking the Law in Africa." The Journal of Pan African Studies 12, no. 5 (November 2018): 108-123.

Silva, Moises. *New International Dictionary of New Testament Theology and Exegesis: Second Edition*. Grand Rapids, MI: Zondervan, 2014.

Smith, Steve. *The Fate of the Jerusalem Temple in Luke-Acts: An Intertextual Approach to Jesus' Laments Over Jerusalem and Stephen's Speech*. London: Bloomsbury T&T Clark, 2017.

Stein, Robert H. *Mark: Baker Exegetical Commentary on the New Testament*. Grand Rapids, MI: Baker Academic, 2008.

Szumskyj, Benjamin John Stephan. "The Role of the Law in the Sanctification of the Believer Today: A Brief Introduction to Pronomianism". Doctoral Dissertation, Liberty University, 2024. Scholars' Crossing.

Talbert, Charles H. *Reading John: A Literary and Theological Commentary on the Fourth Gospel and the Johannine Epistles*. Macon, Georgia: Smyth & Helwys, 2005.

Tawil, Hayim ben Yosef. *Akkadian Lexical Companion for Biblical Hebrew Etymological, Semantic and Idiomatic Equivalence with Supplement on Biblical Aramaic*. New York: Ktav, 2009.

The Apostolic Fathers, Volume I: I Clement. II Clement. Ignatius. Polycarp. Didache. Edited and translated by Bart D. Ehrman. Loeb Classical Library 24. Cambridge, MA: Harvard University Press, 2003.

The Apostolic Fathers, Volume II: Epistle of Barnabas. Papias and Quadratus. Epistle to Diognetus. The Shepherd of Hermas. Edited and translated by Bart D. Ehrman. Loeb Classical Library 25. Cambridge, MA: Harvard University Press, 2003.

Thompson, Alan J. *Exegetical Guide to the Greek New Testament: Luke*. Nashville, TN: B&H Academic, 2016.

Thompson, Marianne Meye. *John: A Commentary*. Louisville, KY: Westminster John Knox, 2015.

Trout, Bradley M. "Matthew 5:17 and Matthew's Community." *Harvard Theological Studies* 72, no. 3 (2016): 1-6.

———. "The Nature of the Law's Fulfilment in Matthew 5:17: An Exegetical and Theological Study." *In die Skrflig* 49, no. 1 (2015): 1-8.

Turner, David L. *Baker Exegetical Commentary on the New Testament: Matthew*. Grand Rapids, MI: Baker Academic, 2008.

Vyhmeister, Nancy Jean, and Terry Dwain Robertson. *Your Guide to Writing Quality Research Papers: For Students of Religion and Theology.* Grand Rapids, MI: Zondervan, 2014.

Wilber, David. *How Jesus Fulfilled the Law: A Pronomian Pocket Guide to Matthew 5:17-20.* Clover, SC: Pronomian Publishing, 2024.

Woodcock, Eldon. "The Filling of the Holy Spirit." *Bibliotheca Sacra* 157, no. 625 (January-March 2000): 68-87.

Young, Brad H. *Jesus the Jewish Theologian.* Grand Rapids, MI: Baker Academic, 1995.

www.ingramcontent.com/pod-product-compliance
Lightning Source LLC
LaVergne TN
LVHW011031110826
845149LV00015B/3377

* 9 7 9 8 9 9 0 8 6 3 0 8 8 *